COOKING
(for A**holes)

COOKING
(for A**holes)

Terrible things I've done.
Tasty apologies.
Little to no remorse.

ZACH GOLDEN

Author of *What the F*@# Should I Make for Dinner?*

Aadamsmedia
Avon, Massachusetts

Published by
Adams Media, a division of F+W Media, Inc.
57 Littlefield Street, Avon, MA 02322. U.S.A.
www.adamsmedia.com

ISBN 10: 1-4405-8073-1
ISBN 13: 978-1-4405-8073-4
eISBN 10: 1-4405-8074-X
eISBN 13: 978-1-4405-8074-1

Printed in the United States of America.

10   9   8   7   6   5   4   3   2   1

Library of Congress Cataloging-in-Publication Data

Golden, Zach.
  Cooking (for a**holes) / Zach Golden.
    pages cm
  ISBN 978-1-4405-8073-4 (paperback) -- ISBN 1-4405-8073-1 (paperback) -- ISBN 978-1-
4405-8074-1 (ebook) -- ISBN 1-4405-8074-X (ebook)
  1. Cooking--Anecdotes. 2. Cooking--Humor. I. Title. II. Title: Cooking for assholes.
  TX652.9.G65 2014
  641.502'07--dc23

                      2014027937

Many of the designations used by manufacturers and sellers to distinguish their products are
claimed as trademarks. Where those designations appear in this book and F+W Media, Inc.
was aware of a trademark claim, the designations have been printed with initial capital letters.

Always follow safety and commonsense cooking protocol while using kitchen utensils, operat-
ing ovens and stoves, and handling uncooked food. If children are assisting in the preparation
of any recipe, they should always be supervised by an adult.

Certain sections of this book deal with activities that would be in violation of various federal,
state, and local laws if actually carried out. We do not advocate the breaking of any law. The
author, Adams Media, and F+W Media, Inc. do not accept liability for any injury, loss, legal
consequence, or incidental or consequential damage incurred by reliance on the information or
advice provided in this book. The information in this book is for entertainment purposes only.

Interior images © THANAWUT MAKAWAN/123RF.

This book is available at quantity discounts for bulk purchases.
For information, please call 1-800-289-0963.

DEDICATION

To Mom, Dad, Jessica, Sara, and Oscar: I'm sorry, sort of.

Contents

INTRODUCTION

Hello, welcome to my book, please take your shoes off (I just vacuumed). You've either purchased, stolen, borrowed, or been gifted this book by a relative that doesn't know you very well; it doesn't matter. What matters is that we're together now. Let's be candid with each other, if only for a moment. *Cooking (for A**holes)* is not my magnum opus; if it were, I'd likely hang myself because let's be honest: We can all do a lot better. So I guess what I'm trying to say is, you're either in store for a mediocre read or one that proves to be my finest work, thereby causing me to question my identity, lose my self-confidence, and fall victim to my own mind before dramatically hanging myself with an Hermès scarf that I bought on credit just to spite American Express, posthumously. Either way, exciting!

When I was a young boy, I was in trouble with great frequency. I had a penchant for fire, and often liked to question adults about the intricacies of their respective genitalia just because it made them appear to be pedophiles or at the very least have poor conversational skills in mixed company. My mother treated me as if I were some sort of Muslin and kept me under constant supervision. I had to shit with the door open until I was five years old. There was not a lot of trust in that relationship. Each afternoon, I'd be forced to sit in the kitchen and watch my mother cook. I'd help by sighing loudly and occasionally throwing something. After a few months of watching, she began to give me small tasks like shelling peas or peeling potatoes and would seem so pleased and proud whenever I completed the simplest of tasks. This was the only time I got that reaction because I was usually fresh off the heels of doing something unspeakably terrible or destructive, or sometimes both.

Even as a little piece-of-shit kid, I learned one of life's most important lessons: If you are ever in the shit, make whoever is mad at you something delicious and they'll forget about all of the terrible things you've done and enjoy your tasty apology. And just to note, you don't actually have to be sorry; this method is a substitute for actually apologizing.

Pats suck. Go Bills.

CHAPTER 1

Work

GRANDPARENT DEATH VACATION

There's a little known loophole in the corporate world: If a loved one dies, you're given "all the time you need" to deal with feelings or whatever. This insulates coworkers from having to think about their own impending deaths by seeing you crying over a Cup-a-Soup alone in the break room because you "just can't believe you'll never see Nana again." And unless you work for the Koch brothers or the WNBA, most employers aren't heartless enough to ask for a death certificate, making this an extremely easy benefit to exploit for anyone with half a conscience or less. In addition, it's not atypical for an adult to have four grandparents, giving you four opportunities to exploit your questionably dead family before you just quit your job and start over.

My grandparents have "died" a combined eleven times, which is impressive because one died three decades before I was birthed, and another years before I learned to lie convincingly. But there's a difference between dying, "dying," and dying. The first refers to the cessation of life; the second refers to deceiving a third party to lead them to believe that someone's life has ceased regardless of fact; and the third refers to a common misspelling of "dyeing," which is the process of altering something's color with a magical substance called dye.

My first post-collegiate job was working at an advertising agency where I wrote really terrible ads for a stool softener brand in exchange for money. Working in advertising is as noble a pursuit as vocational work in the now bourgeoning cat strangling industry, a fact that I learned during my first days on the job. My goals quickly shifted from becoming a contributing member of society by finding a career I could stick to, to spending as little time as humanly possible at the job while still getting paid. But with two weeks of full-time work under my belt, I couldn't take it anymore, so I walked into HR's office and said to nobody in particular, "My grandmother died." Technically, this was true, she had died fourteen years ago, but everyone grieves differently. The important thing to remember is that technically you didn't lie, so there's absolutely no way that you could get in any trouble.

Two weeks later, I returned back from a nice extended paid vacation, and tragedy struck once again. "My grandfather died," I told the stocky HR rep who seemed least dead inside, "probably from grief, he took my grandma's passing pretty hard . . ." Her eyes became glassy but she composed herself and held back the tears. I'm sure later that evening, when recounting the event to one of her seven cats (the one who is the "best listener"), she told Mittens that she had to be "strong, for Zach's sake."

Over the next six months, my two remaining grandparents also "died," resulting in a sum total of twenty-seven days of paid time off during my first seven months of gainful employment. When my last grandparent "died," the HR rep asked for a death certificate, a request she assured me had come from her boss, "who clearly doesn't know what it's like to lose a loved one."

When caught in a lie, you can do one of two things. You can fess up and not make the situation worse, or you can lie more, obscuring the original lie behind an avalanche of random, impossible-to-prove circumstances that only Jack McCoy could untangle. I, of course, opted for the latter, explaining that my grandfather's last wish was for there to be no death certificate because he always felt he had a "mysterious air and this would really ice it." When that lie didn't satiate the HR woman's terrible boss and they demanded the death certificate, I did what any rational person would do and quit because I didn't want to work for a company that doesn't have enough compassion to see I was going through a really difficult time.

Devils on Horseback

Devils on Horseback traditionally uses dates, but you should use prunes so that you can bring up how these "remind you of your grandparents," who you miss so much, and also because they'll give you a nice BM.

24 prunes, pitted
24 salted Marcona almonds
12 slices bacon, halved
½ tablespoon smoked paprika

Preheat your oven to 400°F, and soak 24 toothpicks in a bowl of water. Butterfly the prunes, making damn sure not to slice all the way through. Stuff a Marcona almond inside each prune, then close them back up. Wrap a piece of bacon around each prune, and secure the two ends with a toothpick that you've been soaking in water because you follow directions. Sprinkle with a pinch of smoked paprika, then place on a baking sheet lined with parchment paper. Bake until the bacon is crispy, about 20 minutes. Eat and explain to whoever caught you in a lie that your grandparents all divorced then remarried, so you really have four more potential deaths coming up, you know, just as a heads-up.

CALLING IN SICK

The following is a real e-mail I sent to call out sick because I was just not feeling like working that day.

> To: Redacted
>
> From: Zach Z Golden
>
> Subject: Sick :(
>
>
> Hi team,
>
> I'm not feeling well, so I won't be in the office today. If you need to get in touch with me, I'll be checking my e-mail periodically; otherwise, I should be back in the office soon. "When?" you're probably asking yourselves; well, if all goes well, tomorrow.
>
> If what goes well? Well, I didn't want to burden any of you with the details because it's probably nothing. Less than nothing, if that's possible. It's probably just precautionary. I just went in for a checkup and

my doctor ran a few "very standard tests" as he called them. Anyway, he said something seemed off with my ejaculate (I know this sounds like it's getting risqué, but it's medical; seminal fluids don't always have to be a sexualized thing, guys) so my doctor ordered more tests and then suggested I get a second opinion. He recommended a doctor that was a friend of his, and *that* doctor forced me to ejaculate in front of him so he could check it for whatever was troublesome, and then told me to get out of his car; it was a truly humbling experience. Well, that test came up inconclusive, so *that* doctor referred me to another one of his doctor friends, and he picked me up the next night (by the way, food trucks, mobile bookstores, and now doctor's offices in cars—what a world!) and again, wanted me to ejaculate for him. He also wanted to check my prostate, which was uncomfortable, but luckily he had a station wagon, so we put the seats down and it wasn't as bad as I thought it would be.

Anyway, I had to see another few doctors, each of whom ran their own tests and all of which came back as inconclusive. So that brings me to my appointment today. The cops came across my last appointment and apparently they had never heard of a mobile doctor's office, so they arrested me in a very annoying comedy of errors. I was booked on solicitation, which is as embarrassing as it is ridiculous, and part of the arrest procedure is an HIV test. Long story short I may have tested positive for HIV. It's probably a false positive, or they accidentally switched my blood with that of a gigolo's or something, so it's probably nothing.

Anywho, hopefully I'll see you guys tomorrow. If there's an emergency, call my phone and leave a message. If we've been intimate or shared needles or anything in the past, you should probably make a doctor's appointment. I'm happy to recommend my physician if you're interested.

Cheers,

zg

Chambord Kir Royale

Making coworkers believe you may be HIV positive isn't too bad of a transgression. It's mostly their fault for being so damn nosey; it's like they've never heard of HIPPA. So celebrate not having HIV (hopefully) and say you're sort of sorry with a drink that even children couldn't screw up.

¼ ounce Chambord
Champagne
Raspberry
Twist of lemon

Add the Chambord to a champagne flute, and top with champagne. If you'd like to be extra fancy, garnish each glass with a raspberry and a twist of lemon, and then force the Chambord Kir Royales en masse upon your coworkers until they forget about that thing you did.

EROTIC ASPHYXIATION IS THE SEXIEST ASPHYXIATION

I've always wondered how people get into erotic asphyxiation. Are there informational pamphlets? Is there a group I can join at the YMCA? Are there instructional books on proper erotic safety, filled with diagrams and tutorials that help ensure novice fetishists that they'll experience sexy choking, and not the somewhat less erotic death choking? Erotic asphyxiation, also called autoerotic asphyxiation if you do it in a car, truck, or crossover SUV, restricts the amount of oxygen to your brain, which causes mild hallucinations that apparently make jacking off way more awesome. But there are risks, including injury, death, and most commonly, stretching out a perfectly good scarf to the point of ruin.

After college I was employed by an advertising agency. It was a big company with 400 employees in their New York office. My boss was an egomaniac with the title of Chief Inspiration Officer. He had done a series of somewhat successful ads in the mid-1980s featuring celebrities who have long since overdosed, and was still riding the high from that (and probably lots of cocaine) decades later. He referred to himself as an artist. You were required to remove your shoes before you went in his office because he had gone to a conference in Japan once and wanted to appear worldly. He was immensely unlikeable.

Every Friday at promptly 4:00 P.M., the CIO sent "Inspiration Friday" e-mails to everyone in the company. The contents of these e-mails were thinly veiled humblebrags that showed how cultured and obscure he was. Art openings from artists who ejaculate on news clippings as a form of protest (or to show that they ran out of toilet paper and socks). Bands whose songs were strictly based on Ice-T's monologues from *Law & Order: Special Victims Unit*. He also always managed to mention how his wife was Asian. He didn't meet her on his trip to Japan, but the trip *inspired* him to meet her. And worst of all, he asked that each and every employee at the company reply to his e-mail before they left for the weekend with something that inspires them, so that he can spend his weekend getting inspired, and thusly be the inspirational head of inspiration as the Chief Inspiration Officer of our shitty company.

It was Friday afternoon, and I was presenting to him a series of TV scripts I had written for a very popular fast-food chain. It was not a successful meeting. He didn't find my scripts sufficiently inspirational and the meeting devolved into him taking my computer and showing me things on the Internet that inspired him. He never carried a computer. "I like to think outside the box, so it doesn't make sense to carry one," he said as he logged in to his e-mail to retrieve links. Surprisingly, he didn't sign out.

He apparently did this all of the time. Other employees had experienced the seemingly geriatric lapse in Internet security protocol, and not one of them had done anything about it.

It was 3:57 P.M., so I only had minutes. In his e-mail account I clicked "compose e-mail." I cradled my head in my hands struggling to find my inspiration.

3:58 P.M. I had nothing. I pounded my fists against my desk. It was no use. I pounded them again and again, harder. Each successive blow hurt more than the last, but in a weird way, the pain felt sort of . . . good. Jackpot.

Erotic asphyxiation porn is surprisingly easy to find. It's also deeply disturbing. So as I sent it to all 400 employees from the CIO's e-mail address, just one minute before his weekly 4:00 P.M. e-mails (I didn't want to arouse suspicion), I had this weird feeling in my brain like something was trying to tell me that this was a bad idea. But I ignored it. And it wasn't a bad idea. I wrote, "Now *this* is performance art! My Asian wife and I will be sure to try it this weekend," and included a link to an autoerotic asphyxiation video. And apparently, it was convincing enough that the CIO got fired. I still don't feel bad about this one.

Pigs in a Blanket

Hot dogs are the most commonly choked-upon food item in the world, but unless you're a baby or have a rare medical condition in which you are an adult but have the esophageal physiology of a baby, Pigs in a Blanket should be safe.

1 cup all-purpose flour
1 teaspoon baking powder
¼ teaspoon baking soda
A pinch of salt
3 tablespoons toasted wheat germ

¼ cup chilled vegetable shortening
⅓ cup buttermilk
1 large egg yolk
Miniature frankfurters

Preheat your oven to 375°F and grease a baking sheet. Whisk together the flour, baking powder, baking soda, salt, and wheat germ. Mix in the shortening with a pastry cutter or using your fingertips until the mixture coarsely clumps. In a separate bowl, whisk together the buttermilk and egg yolk, then stir it into the flour mixture until it forms a moist dough. Knead the dough on a floured surface until your forearms hurt and you remember that your New Year's resolution was to exercise more, then pat yourself on the back because technically this counts. Roll the dough to a ¼" thickness and cut it into slightly-less-than-mini-frankfurter-sized strips. Then wrap the pigs in their new blankets and bake for about 15 minutes.

EXCITED TO BE HERE

I worked in advertising for five years. A friend got me a job after I graduated college, and I didn't ever have to interview for it, so at twenty-six years of age, I did not own a suit. It became a point of pride; I was able to have relative success and be a somewhat contributing member of society all while looking like I was walk-of-shaming home from a hobo orgy.

I bought my first suit an hour before my grandfather's funeral because my grandmother felt I looked homeless, and it was a good thing my grandfather was dead; otherwise, he'd be mortified. Had I kept that suit and not dramatically thrown it out minutes after my grandfather's funeral in the Temple lobby garbage can so that I had to ride back to my grandmother's condominium in my underwear, I would have saved myself and my employer from a lot of embarrassment.

To get new clients, ad agencies will be invited to a "pitch," where an agency's C-level executives go to the potential client and present ideas for ad campaigns. From the agencies invited to pitch the company, a winner is chosen, who then gets the business.

I was working on a pitch for Kool-Aid, which my black friends assured me is a wonderful product with great health benefits. The pitch was being led by a Scottish creative director whose breath smelled of whiskey and whose accent was technically another language. It was easier understanding deaf people than it was understanding him, and not the recently deaf, the like, born-this-way deaf. I was a mid-level employee who got high in the handi-capped bathroom every day at 1:00 P.M. and tried not to be noticed. But, being from the great state of New York where folks grow up with a pleasing, genial accent, I was asked to present the work in his stead with three other C-level executives from the company.

The only instruction I was given was to bring a suit and not to get too drunk that night, which is so vague. Too drunk for what? I didn't bring a suit. I didn't own a suit. I just had an old blazer that I bought as a joke in high school and a pair of very form-fitting Twink brand black jeans, which I had washed the night prior.

The next morning, I met my bosses in the lobby ten minutes late. I would have been on time, but I don't know how to use an iron and somehow got my shirt wet trying to use the steam function, so I had to use the iron to dry the shirt, which takes forever. My shirt was mostly dry, but I was more self-conscious about my slacks. They were tight. Really tight. You could see very accurately where my penis and testicles were presently resting, tight. The CEO asked me why I didn't bring a suit and I told him that I didn't own one. I could tell they were worried. He tried to ease the tension and make light of it, forcing laughter as he said, "Well, just don't get an erection."

We took a car over to Kool-Aid's offices. I stared out the window and kept repeating the CEO's words. "Don't get an erection." I had never gotten an embarrassing public erection before, why would I now? But why wouldn't I? What was stopping me? If I didn't, was there something wrong with me? Or my penis? I was experiencing what medical professionals call "the heebie jeebies."

The pitch got underway. My role was simple: sit quietly and then when called upon, read two television scripts; the adults would handle everything else. I didn't hear a word of the pitch; I just kept thinking about the current flaccidity of my penis, assessing and re-assessing it each second. Finally, I was called upon; I began to read the first of the two scripts, but before I could get past the first line, it was requested that I stand so everybody could see and hear me.

I could feel their eyes on me. One by one, their gazes traveled downward to my skin-tight bottom half where I was currently tucked off to the right and hovering around 92 percent flaccidity. I began to read, but soon stopped. Something felt wrong. I felt lightheaded and panicked, so I closed my eyes and took slow, measured breaths for what felt like three seconds. As I found out afterward, it was closer to thirty seconds, during which I closed my eyes, sweated profusely, and became completely, very (very) noticeably erect. We didn't win the pitch.

Purple Drank

Sometimes easing the pain of your indiscretions is best accomplished by literally easing pain, which is what opioids were designed for in the first place. If you don't want to break local, state, or maritime laws, replace the syrup with vodka or gin; it will still get the job done.

2 ounces promethazine with codeine syrup
12 ounces Grape Kool-Aid
Jolly Ranchers

Combine all of the ingredients in a plastic cup or bedazzled goblet. Stir gingerly, then garnish with a Jolly Rancher. Seriously.

A DESCENDANT OF NAZI LEADERSHIP

Adobe Photoshop is a computer program used primarily to superimpose coworkers' heads onto lusciously endowed nude bodies. But Photoshop isn't just a tool for fulfilling previously impossible masturbatory aspirations; you can also manipulate and edit photos, create graphics from scratch, and put strategically placed wieners next to people's mouths in practically any image, so that it appears that they're sucking a big one. Photoshop is both powerful and fairly easy to use for not-old people, making it an important weapon in any terrible human being's arsenal.

I once worked for a man whose last name was Von Richter. To say that he was much maligned by his cohorts would be an understatement tantamount to describing Sir Christopher Cockerell as simply a "smart man" who invented a "useful product." Von Richter's managerial style was so fiercely authoritarian that, coupled with his German heritage and surname, it was often posited that Von Richter was in fact a descendant of Adolf Hitler, or at the very least a high-ranking Nazi official. But Von Richter also had a softer side, as evidenced by the meticulously organized photos hung in a three-row-by-three-column grid on his office wall. Photos of his mother and father, photos of his children, photos of other members of his most likely terrible family. We get it; you have a family, stop showing off, dick.

Von Richter's alleged membership in the Nazi Party began to gather steam around the office. Unbeknownst to him, he became known as the Führer by anyone not named Goebbels, which was the nickname given to his equally horrible assistant. The joke should have stopped there, but thanks to a most likely pirated version of Adobe Photoshop and an inability to discern where the metaphorical (and sometimes actual, I suffer from snow blindness) line is, it didn't.

One day, Von Richter was sick, and it must have been unexpected because the door to his office was left conspicuously ajar. I peered in and I couldn't help mentally comparing myself to Anne Frank as I snuck around silently, looking for some object to call out "manipulate me into a compromising position via an advanced computer software program." And there it was, in Alice Nelson's position on the grid of photos: a young Von Richter bouncing happily on his father's knee.

After some tinkering and placing dongs around baby and father Von Richter's mouths, I settled upon superimposing an exuberant baby Von Richter, smiling to show his one useless tooth interrupting an otherwise gummy smile, bouncing gleefully on Adolf Hitler's knee while his father stood on watching in admiration. I replaced the framed photo with the enhanced version, hung it back on the wall, and then called the company's anonymous whistleblower's hotline because as a Jew, I was offended by this blatantly hurtful imagery.

The next day the Führer was back in the office. He asked to speak to me. "You know the young people in the office, who do you think would have done this?" I told him I hadn't the faintest, and that it was a good thing they didn't have security cameras, otherwise somebody, much like Lucy, would have some explaining to do. Either Von Richter didn't understand my clever wordplay, or he was truly hurt, because his eyes became glassy and tears were imminent. Being in the presence of an adult male crying is appropriate only at funerals, or while watching the last few scenes of *Rudy*, so I said the only thing I could think of: "You must admit, that is some pretty solid Photoshop work." He agreed.

Potato Latkes

You're not just making latkes, a food made famous by Jews who felt that pancakes were too extravagant; you're showing whomever you accused of contributing to genocide that you don't believe that they actually participated in the atrocity by preparing a dish popularized by "not" their enemy (it's also a test; if they refuse the food, they are definitely Nazi sympathizers).

1 pound russet potatoes, peeled and
  grated
½ cup grated onion
1 large egg, lightly beaten
1 tablespoon flour

1 teaspoon salt
½–¾ cup schmaltz
Sour cream
Applesauce

Peel and grate your potatoes and onion, then put them in cheesecloth or a dishtowel and wring out as much of the moisture as humanly possible, then curse your God for making you too weak to adequately remove all the moisture. Blame It on the Jews, if you don't like smiting God. Transfer the mixture to a bowl, and stir in the egg, flour, and salt. Heat the schmaltz in a sauté pan over medium-high heat until hot. If you can't find schmaltz, don't know what schmaltz is, or are adverse to strangling a chicken in order to make your own schmaltz, canola oil works nicely, too. Cook latkes for 5 minutes per side, until each side is crispy and brown, then season with a pinch of salt and enjoy. Serve with sour cream, applesauce, and a sense of frugality.

CHAPTER 2

Friends

GIRLS DEFINITIVELY POOP

Whoever invented the preposterous "girls don't poop" pseudo-myth must have had a very dim view of women. In an unpublished early copy of Abraham Maslow's "A Theory of Human Motivation," regular poops was the highest level of his hierarchy of needs, above self-actualization and "getting it on the regular." If I don't poop for two days, it's all I can think about, so if women never pooped, they would be heinous, unspeakably terrible creatures (which they're not, mostly).

Since I was able to know anything, I've known that girls poop. Growing up, my mom's best friend had a little girl who was the same age as me, and when we were very little we'd get baths together. And despite being about two years old, one of my earliest memories is that girl pooping in the bath because you don't forget that, ever. And though this childhood trauma taught me the truth, it didn't stop girls from perpetuating the lie even decades later.

Toward the end of high school, a friend's girlfriend was still holding on to this little nugget of untruth. She would defend it with the evangelical flair of a homeschooled child, despite everyone around her knowing well beyond a reasonable doubt that girls do in fact poop. Even with her boyfriend of two years, when she went to the bathroom, she would turn on the faucet or shower to obscure the sound of her tears (and ostensible doody noises), then liberally mist a lemon spray and stay in the bathroom for five to ten minutes until any olfactory evidence had disappeared.

I'm unable to sit by and let someone be willfully wrong, especially about a topic I'm so passionate about. And after two years of listening to this pathological nonsense, I couldn't take it anymore. So when the entirety of our senior class boarded four charter buses en route to Montréal, I acted.

The funny thing about Ex-Lax is that they make it chocolate flavored. And perhaps to disparage the notion that you were taking medicine, which is icky, they make the little dosage bars look remarkably like chocolate bars, except for the embossed Ex-Lax moniker on each piece. I found that rubbing the bars of Ex-Lax against the floor of a bus is an effective method in removing such an embossment, leaving the medicine looking indistinguishable from a chocolate bar. And as it turns out, little Miss Poop Denier was a self-professed chocoholic, which made sense because she seemed predisposed to addiction.

I'll put it this way: After that bus ride, every single person on that bus knew with absolute certainty that girls poop. A charter bus bathroom is only designed to handle a finite amount of waste, and when that threshold has been met, you have what is called backlog. We reached the backlog stage around hour two of the seven-hour trip, and kept chugging along. And while the poop denier was embarrassed, I bet she also felt liberated now that she didn't have to hang on to her lie. And on top of being liberated, she probably also felt quite emptied, because man did that girl shit.

GINGER OLD-FASHIONED

If you're going to induce diarrhea or any other stomach malady, you should have the god-damned common courtesy to help soothe it, too. Ginger is known to calm the stomach and put an end to unsightly episodes of diarrhea. It's also a fun term for light-skinned, red-headed people who should be chemically or manually castrated to avoid reproduction.

1"-ish piece of candied ginger
1 ounce blood orange bitters
1 ounce seltzer water
Maraschino cherry
Ice to fill an old-fashioned glass
1 ounce rye whiskey
Orange slice

Muddle the ginger, blood orange bitters, a splash of seltzer, and a maraschino cherry. Add the ice, rye, and another splash of seltzer. Stir with much vim and perhaps also vigor. Garnish with a slice of orange and make yourself one because you earned it.

OF RIBS AND LIES

Living with friends is almost universally a bad idea. You don't want to mix the people you love, who are a respite from everything that gives you the urge to punch old ladies, what with their stupid hats, and the people you silently hate because they won't pick their goddamn hair out of the shower drain. The hate and contempt that bubble under the veneer of "best friends forever" and "Hey, this is totally better than living with some rapist off Craigslist" is enough to turn anyone into a terrible person.

This knowledge is, unfortunately, not secondhand. I conducted primary research by sharing a 550-square-foot apartment with a friend, Todd, for two years. Two years of dirty dishes piled high in the sink, trash overflowing from the garbage can, and wet towels mildewing on the bathroom floor. And after two years of me silently hating him for treating me like a small Hispanic woman who comes in for two hours per week to tidy up, I was done. In addition to being done, I was also hungry, so I went to the fridge, where I discovered a cardboard takeout container bearing the markings of Dinosaur Bar-B-Que, the greatest restaurant in the world. I should mention, in addition to being quite unsanitary in his living habits, my roommate also had a girlfriend who spent seven nights per week and frequently as many days in our apartment, despite having her own apartment that I'm sure her parents paid for because she was terrible.

"Don't eat that, I brought it home for Todd," said the terrible girlfriend. Thankfully, she disappeared back into Todd's room, where I assume she sacrificed small animals or mailed letters laced with ricin just because it made her feel powerful. Well, those ribs were the most delicious ribs I have ever eaten. Smoky, juicy, porky perfection. Twenty minutes into my post-meal sedation, my roommate returned home. He was in a good mood, rubbing his hands together as he walked to the kitchen, as if to warm them over a fire. I heard the refrigerator door open, then nothing. He yelled to his terrible girlfriend, calling her "Babe," which is only not annoying if you're talking to a pig in the city. She emerged from her Tatooine lair, and after a very unthorough inspection of the refrigerator, she accused me of eating the ribs. Now, technically, she was correct, but I wasn't about to let this large collection of human garbage accuse me of something, even if I did it.

I was asked to provide an alternate theory to the crime. "I don't know, maybe somebody took them when I was taking the garbage out since it was overflowing . . ." They didn't buy that, but I'd like to think I got my point across. After several more minutes of accusations and my artful dodging of them, the terrible girlfriend receded back into Todd's bedroom. We sat alone in the living room. He asked me to come clean so we could just move past it. So I said the first thing that popped into my head. "Your girlfriend tried to have sex with me. She forced herself on me."

She didn't. But suddenly, the ribs were insignificant. It was perfect, except that instead of instantly walking into his bedroom and throwing out his terrible girlfriend without any explanation, he began to ask questions. "When did this happen?" "How could you do this to me?" And after the question phase, came statements. "I just bought her a ring." And "But we have a cat together."

He walked slowly to his bedroom like he had just seen death. There were raised voices and audible sobbing. A few minutes later, the couple emerged from the bedroom. They appeared unified, and as the terrible girlfriend refuted my accusation, things became increasingly heated. When asked what exactly she did to try and have sex with me, my answer did not provide comfort to my friend. "I don't know, she just kind of has that DTF vibe." There was more yelling after that.

"We want you to move out," they said.

"Well, technically, I'm the one on the lease, so . . ."

We were in the puzzling situation of me being too stubborn to move out, and them being too poor to move out, so I said it (but I didn't mean it). "I'm sorry." Honestly, they were less touched than I thought they'd be. They kept focusing on the fact that I had lied in the first place, which my apology should have erased, but clearly nobody taught them manners, or to take out the goddamn trash.

RIBS

Much like God, assholes have the power to giveth and taketh away. And when you taketh away stuff from people, it's best to giveth back to them to apologize. So if taketh away food, cooketh whatever you tooketh away, or something.

¼ cup packed dark brown sugar plus 2 tablespoons dark brown sugar,
   divided
3 teaspoons salt, divided
1½ teaspoons black pepper, divided
2 tablespoons paprika
1½ teaspoons chipotle chili powder
1½ teaspoons ground cumin
2 racks pork spareribs, St. Louis cut
1 large onion, chopped
6 garlic cloves, finely chopped
1½ tablespoons fresh ginger, peeled and finely chopped
2 tablespoons sunflower oil
1½ cups ketchup
½ cup apple cider vinegar
6 tablespoons soy sauce
½ cup water

Preheat the oven to 350°F. Mix the 2 tablespoons brown sugar, 1½ teaspoons salt, 1 teaspoon pepper, and spices together in a small bowl. Line a sheet tray with aluminum foil and brush on some oil. Pat your ribs dry and put them on the sheet tray. If they are wet, you might as well just throw them in the garbage and tell whomever you're cooking for that you hate them because the spice rub won't adhere properly and they'll be terrible. Rub the ribs all over with the spice mixture, cover them with foil, and then bake on the center rack of your oven for 80 minutes, no more, no less. While they're baking, make the sauce. Sauté the onion, garlic, and ginger in the sunflower oil over high heat for 6 minutes. Add the ketchup, apple cider vinegar, soy sauce, water, and remaining brown sugar, salt, and pepper.

Simmer for 15 minutes, then purée it all up in a blender or use an immersion blender until smooth. Get your grill going and cook the ribs on a sheet tray over indirect heat for 40 minutes, basting with sauce every 10 minutes. Don't burn yourself, or if you do, just know that it wasn't my fault. Rest your meat for at least 10 minutes before eating. If you skip resting, I will injure you and make it look like an accident.

STABBED IN THE BACK

The average middle school houses more assholes than any other structure (except, of course, for any government building). All youths are assholes. And many teachers are assholes. But the biggest asshole in any middle school is always the same; it's the gym "teacher." Who grows up, goes to college, and decides, hey, you know what, I'm going to watch kids play dodge ball for the next forty years? Two groups: pedophiles and assholes, and pedophiles are basically assholes, just with a more, shall we say, niche attraction, so you get the point.

In my middle-school gym class, each semester we would have to complete a physical fitness test, essentially an ad hoc separator of athletes vs. fatties. You would partner up and record one another's scores as it pertained to sit-ups, pull-ups, pushups, sprints, jump ropes, and of course, running a single mile. Being the type of person to not take "physical education" seriously, my friend Ben and I partnered up, complicit in doctoring one another's scores to make it appear that we were superior athletes despite minimal effort. And so on the final day of the physical fitness test, after four previous in which by all accounts I was a model student, my true colors shone brightly.

We were on to sit-ups. Ben was powering through the first thirty seconds, and with the hypnotic pendulum of his torso flying up and down, my mind drifted. All that lay on the blue mat were pieces of paper, detailing each student's scores, and pencils to record them, one would think. After a brief, albeit comprehensive, internal argument about the durability of our pencil (and pencils in general), I concluded that placing a pencil upright below my friend's undulating back would result in it snapping comically, much to the delight of both of us, and the admiration of our fellow students. However, an asshole's mind often stops at the desired outcome, quickly skipping over the more painful realities, much like that of an irresponsible child.

As he rose up, I took my chance, sliding the pencil into place and holding it eraser side up (if things went wrong, I didn't want him to get lead poisoning, which was really a foregone conclusion seeing as pencils have used graphite for the better part of a century). He whipped back down and I listened for the comical snap of wood, but instead heard only the pained screams of my closest friend, forgetting about his sit-up-related duties and now focusing his attention on the foot-long cut on his back.

I was quickly ushered to the vice-principal's office, where I managed to escape suspension by mustering fake tears (pro tip: pinch your testicles through your pocket for convincing agony), but was still handed down a week of detention "to think about what I had done." Ben was okay; the nurse bandaged him up and he was good as new. In that week of detention I did think about what I had done, and I realized that my logic was flawed. If I wanted the pencil to snap comically, I should have put the eraser side down so that it would have a stable base. I've got to hand it to the vice-principal; I really did learn my lesson.

SWORDFISH WITH PINK PEPPERCORNS AND PRESERVED LEMON

Humans are conditioned to react based upon past experiences. And when those experiences are negative, as a result of something terrible you've done, it's your responsibility to create positive associations. So if your friend equates stabbing with something negative, cook him swordfish and he'll be all better. You can't argue with science.

¼ cup butter, softened
1 tablespoon fresh parsley, chopped
2 cloves garlic, minced
2 teaspoons whole pink peppercorns
1 teaspoon preserved lemon peel, finely chopped

Salt
1 tablespoon olive oil
Fresh black pepper
4 swordfish steaks

Preheat the oven to 400°F. Throw the softened butter, parsley, garlic, pink peppercorns, and preserved lemon in a bowl. Mix together until everything is incorporated and smooth, then season to taste with salt. If you don't have preserved lemons, you can use grated lemon peel, but the dish will be less good, and your apology will be less sincere. Heat the oil in a sauté pan over high heat. Season the swordfish with salt and black pepper, then sauté until browned, about 3 minutes. Turn the swordfish over and roast in the oven for about 10 minutes, or until it's just cooked through. Remove from the oven and mount the fish with the compound butter, which sounds sexual, but unfortunately isn't. To mount, just add the butter to the hot pan and spoon it over the swordfish steaks until the butter is all melted. Spoon the pan sauce over the swordfish steaks and let the healing begin.

SHIT

Terrible people make terrible friends. And not just for the obvious reasons (inability to prioritize the needs of others above their own, fondness of fire, difficulty achieving climax without the pain and suffering of others, etc.). To a truly terrible person, a friend is just a patsy that keeps coming back.

When you're friends with a terrible person, one minute you're living your life and everything's great and the next there is non-metaphorical, literal shit in the bathtub. It wasn't my fault, really. I was fifteen years old, not a boy, not yet a man, and my best friend, Dan, had joined me at a summer camp on a glacier in Oregon, where white people could ski and snowboard all summer long. It was only a few days into our session, but I still hadn't been able to achieve a thorough elimination, likely due to the fact that airplanes are the Medusa to my bowels and I had flown across the country just three days earlier.

My father only has one piece of advice. It doesn't matter the situation; it's an all-encompassing solution to all of life's problems. Dad, I like this girl, but I don't know how to tell her. Dad, my car is currently aflame. Dad, I went to school in blackface, but people didn't get it and now I'm being chased. His answer was always the same: "Why don't you try a glycerin suppository?"

So I did. And I waited. And waited. And I danced in place until I couldn't wait anymore. And then in a cacophony of relieved grunting and barnyard impressions, it was over. Suddenly, my dad's advice made sense. Everything was wonderful. I felt like dancing.

I flushed with great optimism, but the mass lazily circled the bowl, rising rather than descending. I panicked and grabbed the plunger, thrusting it into the toilet with desperate stabs. When I dared to open my eyes, the water was receding.

I held the plunger up in victory and for the first time noticed that I've never seen this type of plunger before. Rather than a rubber cup at the end of a wooden rod, it was a large accordion-shaped design. I examined it inquisitively, admiring its efficacy while wondering how it works; it literally seemed to make my excrement disappear. But before I could employ the scientific method to form a hypothesis, test it, and analyze it, the entirety of my waste released from the accordion plunger, landing with a dull thud like a piece of steak falling on linoleum in the bathtub. My hypothesis is that this was some sort of novelty plunger used for pranking friends into spreading their feces around the house. It seemed like a small market product, but clearly it had its niche.

I had to think fast. Thanks to my father and Dulcolax brand glycerin suppositories, I had only been in the bathroom for roughly thirty seconds. I was faced with a choice: to have to touch human waste or blame it on someone else.

"Oh my God, somebody that wasn't me shit in the bathtub!" I threw open the door, screaming in disgust. The counselor ran to the bathroom to assess the situation. His eyes grew in horror and he began stuttering like a young child with a comical developmental delay, "Wh-wh-wh-wh-who was in there before you?"

At that moment, Dan walked into the cabin. The counselor and I turned in unison, eyes locked on Dan. "It smells like shit in here," he said.

"It was him," I said.

"Did you use this bathroom before Zach?" the counselor asked.

"Yes. So?"

"I'm really disappointed in you." This was something that was said to me dozens of times in my life, so it felt odd to say to another person. He protested, but the evidence against him was overwhelming, and in the end, Dan cleaned up my feces. It wasn't a total loss for him though; he became known around camp as "Shit in the Tub Dan," which he didn't like but I felt suited him considering the situation.

PUMPKIN SOUP WITH FRIED SAGE

Pumpkin is a powerful natural defense against diarrhea, or as it's known medically, Mud Butt. So if you are engaging in activities that may result in you, or the people around you, acquiring diarrhea, know how to protect against it, deliciously.

1 small (~5-pound) pie pumpkin
4 tablespoons olive oil
6 slices bacon, diced
2 onions, diced
2 cloves garlic, minced
Salt and pepper
4 cups chicken stock
½ cup canola oil
18 sage leaves

Preheat your oven to 350°F. Quarter your pumpkin, remove the seeds, rub it sensually with olive oil, and bake it on a sheet tray for 40 minutes. In a large stockpot, add the bacon over medium-high heat and sauté for 4 minutes. Add the onion, garlic, salt, and pepper and cook for another 8 minutes, stirring occasionally. Scrape the flesh from the pumpkin and add it to the stockpot, then add the chicken stock and simmer for 30 minutes. Purée the mixture until smooth. In a small pan, heat the canola oil until very hot. Add the sage leaves and fry until crispy, and then drain on a paper towel and season with salt and pepper. Serve the soup topped with the fried sage, a drizzle of olive oil, and the knowledge that your butthole is on the mend.

BERNIE LOVE

One of my closest, most dear friends in the entire world was dating a monster. We had known each other since we were seven. Our fathers were friends so we were forced to be so, but we remained friends long after our fathers' falling out over splitting a bill in '93 (my father felt that if you have the gall to order the most expensive thing on the menu *and* be the only one to order dessert, the rest of the table shouldn't have to subsidize your meal, you goddamn freeloader). Now, the closest thing I had in the world to a brother was having his spirit ripped from him by this terrible girlfriend.

Amongst our friends, the distaste for this girl was unanimous. My friend assured us that she's different when the two of them are alone, but we drilled holes in his bedroom walls and spied on them, and it was conclusively determined that she was the same awful person alone as she was in public. Then, after finding the holes, she tried to get us in trouble with the police because we installed hidden cameras in *our* friend's room so that we could more effectively study their time together in order to prove conclusively the veracity of *our* friend's statement. She was jealous, passive-aggressive, and woefully insecure. A roommate of ours who was three years away from a psychology degree posited that she met the clinical definition of someone with borderline personality disorder. We all urged our friend to break up with this horrid bog-monster.

They had been dating for six months. I knew this because my friend kept talking about his plans for their six-month anniversary, which is apparently a thing that weak men celebrate. He pulled me into his bedroom and closed the door, peeking out from the crack of the doorway to make sure nobody was spying on us (we were; we said we took the cameras out but did not). He lifted the corner of his mattress and produced a small box; inside was a pretty poor attempt at an engagement ring. He said he was going to propose. I told him he was making the biggest mistake of his life. He politely disagreed and asked for my support.

That night, we threw him a party. We told him it was a pre-engagement bachelor party because that sounds as real as a six-month anniversary. We bought lots of alcohol, invited a bevy of women, and set out a tasteful crudité platter. It was going to be a grand soirée, and the best part was, his terrible girlfriend wasn't invited.

We managed to get the fiancé-to-be very inebriated. He passed out sitting upright on the couch. I made a *Weekend at Bernie's* joke and every single person at the party, and a few who weren't at the party, laughed and commended me on my wit and also handsomeness.

My genius joke sparked an equally genius idea; I found a girl with naturally low inhibitions, and after very little persuasion, she agreed to kiss my friend. We grabbed him by his shirt, propping him upright, much like Terry Kiser expertly playing Bernie Lomax, and I surreptitiously snapped photo after photo of this impromptu forced romance, which made me feel like James Bond except that I can't drink martinis because I get a tummy ache. The next morning, in a plain manila envelope labeled "Cunt," printouts of those photos were silently slipped under his girlfriend's door by a dashing, unnamed lad. Later that day, I got a call from a devastated friend. He was in tears and I was barely able to hear or tolerate him. But through his tears and disgusting crying, I could make out one thing with perfect clarity: "She said no." Well, yeah, obviously, you cheated on her, you monster.

LISTENING COCKTAIL

When you are forced to ruin someone's life for his and/or her own good, it's important to be there for that person afterward. Unless you don't like him or her; then get out of there lickety-split.

1 bottle of vodka
2 ears
1 heart

Drink the vodka, pretend to listen to what your friend is saying, reassure your friend that the terrible thing you've done will somehow lead to a positive outcome, and repeat until it's all better.

CHAPTER 3

(in)Significant Others

LOVE IS JUST A FOUR-LETTER WORD

Jealousy is kind of like a butthole; everyone has it, and 100 percent of the time, it's really gross. I'm guilty of it, too. Every time Sir Christopher Cockerell's name is mentioned in conversation, my life seems unimportant and insignificant compared to his great accomplishments; with my great respect comes great jealousy. For some, it breeds motivation, in others hatred and self-loathing, and in the case of my college girlfriend, it bred psychosis and a ringing sound in her ears that would later be diagnosed as tinnitus.

I'm not saying that all women are crazy when jealous; that would be an unfounded, sweeping generalization. I am, however, saying that all of the women that I've *met* are turned crazy when jealous; there's a big difference. None were crazier than an ex-girlfriend of mine named Hilary (unfortunately not Clinton; by the way, did she get elected president? It's 2014, when is it where you are?). Hilary was a wonderful, sweet, conscientious girl when sober. But as soon as she starting getting crunk, as was the fashion at the time, her inner personality disorder would come out. So it probably wasn't a good sign that we met at a bar, spent most of our time together at a bar, and consummated our like for each other for the first time in a bar bathroom.

If a bar had a female bartender, I would get chewed out for talking to her when I bought Hilary drinks, which she insisted upon because "I was the hotshot with a job." And if a girl ever smiled at me, made the mistake of engaging in polite conversation, or unintentionally brushed against me in a crowded tavern, Hilary would have to be restrained by three people because she had PCP strength when jealous.

Above all else, the thing that made her most angry was that I didn't get as jealous as she did; that killed her. One night, at some bar in Brooklyn, a devilish young lad in a Buffalo Bills T-shirt decided to try his luck with Hilary, obviously unaware that I, a man who loves the Buffalo Bills more than many members of my family, was currently non-exclusively dating her reluctantly. He offered to buy her a drink, and rather than answering him, Hilary grabbed me and said, "I have a boyfriend, you asshole." She pushed me toward him.

"Are you a Bills fan?" I asked.

"Until the day I die. I'm from Orchard Park, you?" He was delightful.

"Rochester." I wonder if he's looking for friends.

"Excuse me, he tried hitting on me." Hilary didn't realize that men were talking. "You need to fight him."

I most certainly did not fight him. In fact, Hilary's words only lent credence to what my gut was telling me. I needed to just put myself out there, allow myself to feel vulnerable, and go for it. "Hey man, I don't want this to be weird, but could I get your number and maybe we could watch a Bills game together sometime?"

"Sure thing. I usually just get high and order wings during the game." He was magnificent. Hilary didn't agree, and gave me an ultimatum: "Him or me." I chose him. We had more in common.

BUFFALO WINGS

Sometimes an apology is not for being a terrible person, but for cavorting with them. If you spend time around assholes, you're going to get shit on, so just remember: If you bring assholes around, their misdeeds are on you.

24 chicken wings
Vegetable oil
1 cup Frank's RedHot Sauce
1 stick butter
1½ tablespoons white vinegar
¼ teaspoon Worcestershire sauce
¼ teaspoon cayenne pepper
⅛ teaspoon garlic powder
Blue cheese dressing
Celery, cut into 4" batons
Carrots, cut into 4" batons

99.9 percent of the world fucks up Buffalo Wings. There are two important rules: 1. Don't bread the wings or coat them in flour, ever, and 2. If you bake your wings, close this book, take a long hard look at your life, and ask yourself where you went wrong.

Fry the wings in vegetable oil at 350°F for 10 to 12 minutes, then drain. In a saucepan, combine the Frank's, butter, vinegar, Worcestershire sauce, cayenne pepper, and garlic powder, stirring until smooth. Place the wings and sauce in a sealed container and shake vigorously. Serve with blue cheese dressing, celery, and carrots, and never ranch dressing. Never.

THE LESSON OF PHEIDIPPIDES

Marathons are stupid, and anybody that puts a 26.2 sticker on his car is a terrible person. The first person to run a marathon was a Greek messenger named Pheidippides, who ran from the battlefield of Marathon all the way to Athens just to announce, and I'm paraphrasing here, "We beat the Persians! Which reminds me, why do they insist upon being called Persians and not Iranians? Does that bother anyone else?" Then, he dropped dead from exhaustion. The first person to ever run a marathon literally died as a result of it, and somehow, it was decided that this death-race should become a thing that white people do to raise money for charities that "are like, really important, guys."

I had a girlfriend who really wanted me to run a marathon. We would go to parties and she'd introduce me: "This is my boyfriend, Zach. He's training for a marathon." But I wasn't; running is a punishment, not a sport. One day she texted me, "I have a special surprise for you tonight . . ." I was pretty sure this was a thinly veiled allusion to anal sex. It was not. She had signed me up for a marathon and felt "like, really strongly, that you do it."

The proper marathon training routine involves running five days a week, gradually increasing and varying the distances. I opted for walking to a video game store near my house and playing the two-quarter demo of Madden for Xbox 360 until I thought a convincing amount of time had passed and

I could go home to my girlfriend who I was afraid of, or the dick assistant manager Marcus kicked me out.

Finally, race day was upon us. She dropped me at the starting line, helped me get my bib, and said she would wait for me at the finish line, wearing a T-shirt with my name and face on it, which was less of a turn-on than I thought it would be.

When she was out of sight, I left and spent the next two hours drinking, smoking weed, and trying cocaine for the first and then second time. Then I had a friend drive me to one mile from the finish line, where I snuck down a side street, ducked the crowd, and began running toward the finish. Hindsight will say that I should have at least done an Internet search for "marathon" so I could learn the basics, like etymology and how long it takes the average person to complete the race, but as they say, hindsight is only for Pagans.

The crowd became excited and started looking at their watches. Some began running, following me from behind the police barriers as I raced to the finish. The crowd was going crazy, cheering, looking up at the clock as I jogged. I finished with a time of 1:58:32, which apparently is very good.

My girlfriend was crying tears of joy. She ran up and kissed me, screaming with hilarious passion. But then one of the hundreds of people who saw me cheat snitched, and after a bunch of white people huddled, I was disqualified. We broke up, right then and there. She said I humiliated her, and when I looked at her, wearing a T-shirt with my face on it, I realized she was wrong. She humiliated herself.

NOT GROSS ENERGY BARS

In the rare instance that you're not in the wrong, apologize to yourself. Most energy bars are gross and for terrible people who wear a bike jersey for a ride around the neighborhood. But, they can also give you the energy to survive terrible people. Also, they're chewy, so if things get really bad, give them to whoever is annoying you and who knows, maybe they'll choke to death.

2 cups Medjool dates, pitted and chopped
2 cups raw cashews
½ cup raw almonds, skinned
¾ cup cocoa powder
Pinch of sea salt
½ cup shredded coconut
½ cup mini milk chocolate chips
2 tablespoons vanilla extract
½ teaspoon almond extract
3 tablespoons cold water

Add the dates, cashews, almonds, cocoa powder, and sea salt into a food processor. Pulse until the texture is coarse. Add the shredded coconut, chocolate chips, vanilla extract, and almond extract. Add the water a little bit at a time, until it holds together as a moist dough. Scrape the mixture into a square cake pan lined with aluminum foil, smooth it out evenly, and chill the mixture for at least an hour before slicing.

FIRST DATE

My uncle Donnie met his second of four wives during a bank robbery. He was just minding his business, arguing with a teller about an overdraft fee, when all of a sudden four masked men brandished guns and yelled for everyone to lie on the ground, no funny business. It was quite the ordeal, too, a fourteen-hour hostage standoff until a SWAT team came in and killed the robbers, thereby ensuring a happy ending. Seeing how shell-shocked the beautiful young teller appeared, Uncle Donnie invited her out to dinner. Donnie isn't much of a looker, and as bad as he is to look at, he's even worse to spend time with, but nonetheless, the beautiful teller accepted the invitation. That night they bonded in their trauma, and afterward had absolutely consensual sex (don't listen to the rumors; they're untrue).

When I was in fifth grade, I had my first schoolboy crush. Uncle Donnie told me the story of his second wife, and left me with this advice: Experience something traumatic together and you'll be bonded forever, or at least for a while, which is just as good.

We went on our first date on February 1, 1993. I know that because I still have the newspaper clipping from the next day with the headline "Children Narrowly Escape Death."

Uncle Donnie helped me brainstorm some possibly traumatic date ideas. Upstate New York, being relatively safe, was limited on options, so we settled on a train tracks picnic, one of Old Uncle Donnie's standbys. He helped me pack a picnic basket and even bought us a six-pack of Genny Cream Ale, and then he dropped us near a heavily rusted railroad bridge crossing the Erie Canal.

We dined and would have drank the beers Donnie bought us, but we didn't have a bottle opener or ingenuity, apparently, and were thwarted. It was a nice date, very innocent; when our eyes met, she couldn't help but smile and look shyly away.

The tracks began to vibrate slightly, then over the next minute, with increasing frequency and amplitude. In the distance, a train inched toward us, still small on the horizon. We gathered our things and began to move to safety, but I noticed that we had left six bottles of beer on the tracks.

Uncle Donnie had been very specific: If I wasn't going to drink the booze, save it for him. Never waste good booze; he said it all the time. I climbed back toward the tracks and my date followed me, unwilling to let me face danger alone. The train appeared larger. Its horn rang loud with three shrill blasts. We grabbed the bottles and headed back, the train still at a safe distance. I climbed down the bridge, but my date didn't follow. She was yelling my name with increasing panic. She was stuck.

I carefully set the bottles down and ran to her, trying to help her dislodge her foot from the track. She was wearing Teva brand sports sandals and one of the useless, ill-designed, poorly conceived Velcro straps was stuck between two pieces of metal on the track's edge. The train held its horn, much louder now. There was a sharp gust of wind in our faces and the train's brakes rang loud but did little to slow the train down.

We discussed the impracticality of sports sandals, then I was able to cut the strap with a pocket knife, freeing her. I couldn't hear; the train shook everything around us as it reached the bridge. I grabbed her and jumped with all of my might.

For a moment, I felt nothing. I closed my eyes and felt water surround me. The train had missed us and we jumped safely into the canal below. My date was crying hysterically. I was crying hysterically. She clung to me in the dirty canal water, holding her body tightly against mine. She kept thanking me and telling me I saved her life, but I was more focused on the fact that through her T-shirt, I was pretty sure I could see her nipples. All in all, a pretty successful first date.

BEER-BRAISED PORK

If you are responsible for traumatizing someone, remember that you are the puppet master and he or she is the puppet, so do with that what you will. It's best to avoid forcing your victims to relive their trauma, unless of course you do it through food; then you can just chalk it up to being a coinkydink and not come off as a monster.

4 pounds-ish pork shoulder
2 tablespoons chili powder
1 tablespoon dark brown sugar
1 tablespoon garlic powder
2 teaspoons salt
A lot of fresh black pepper
2 dried guajillo chilies
2 cans Negra Modelo lager
4 garlic cloves, crushed

At least 3 hours before, and you should really do it overnight, rub the pork shoulder with the chili powder, brown sugar, garlic powder, salt, and pepper and refrigerate. Toast the chilies in a dry cast-iron pot over medium heat for about 2 minutes. Remove the stems and seeds and cut them in half. Preheat your oven to 500°F, put the pork in a roasting pan, then roast it for 45 minutes. Add the beer, chilies, and garlic and cover with aluminum foil. Reduce the heat to 350°F and cook until the meat is tender and shreds easily, about 2 hours.

MY SUPER HOT ASIAN GIRLFRIEND

I like to think I see the good in people. I'm an optimist, a glass-is-half-full kind of guy. When I was dating, I'd see the good in that person for precisely three weeks, and then I'd finally see all of the terrible stuff that everyone else saw and I'd break up with her because I could never be with a monster like that. Then I would find another someone just like that person and repeat. That constant cycle of short-term mahogany meant that I never really had to meet the parents. In fact, if they even mentioned their parents, I was out of there. No parents, never again.

A Freudian psychologist would likely say that a traumatic event from my childhood manifests itself in what seems like a compulsive desire to undermine all of my relationships before they can become serious, and that I want to have sex with my mother. He was right about one of those things.

My senior year of high school, I dated the girl of my dreams. She was Asian and had pretty big tits for an Asian, and she loved performing fellatio, which may or may not have to do with her being Asian; I'm not an expert. Our love for each other was real. We dated for a month and then she invited me to dinner with her parents (who were also Asian, in case you were wondering). I accepted, excited to be taking the next step in our relationship. It just felt right, much like her larger than average–sized Asian breasts (with nice nipples, too).

When I arrived, the whole family answered the door. Mom, Dad, my hot Asian girlfriend, and her two brothers, all of them Asian. We had fajitas, which at the time I thought was an Asian delicacy but it's not; I checked, guys. They were a lovely family, supportive of one another in every way. They respected everyone's opinion no matter how it differed from their own. These were good people. I felt accepted; they were easy to talk to, listened intently, and seemed to find whatever I said very interesting. They also offered wise, well-thought-out advice that felt not at all judge-y, just like they really cared. And, their daughter was still super hot, and super Asian. Huge tits, too.

After dinner, I excused myself to the bathroom. I had a normal elimination. I didn't even watch after I flushed to make sure all was clear; I just confidently washed my hands and fake-boxed the handsome devil in the mirror with the super hot Asian girlfriend with the giant tits. Now I don't know if Asians and white Jewish people are physiologically different (I mean aside from the eyes, obviously). I'm not a doctor or a scientist, but my best guess is that they definitely are because their toilet clearly had never handled a white Jew–sized poop before.

This buffoon of a toilet began to overflow, depositing feces and water on the floor of the Asian family's impeccably and tastefully renovated bathroom. The water wouldn't stop, and as part of their tasteful renovation, the water shut-off valve was located behind a surreptitious panel on the wall, which I did not find. The water ran out of the bathroom and into the hallway. After a minute, my fucking smoking hot Asian girlfriend with the monster cans' parents knocked on the door, asking if I needed help. They sounded sincere and nonjudgmental. At least I think they did, I was already one foot out the window because I was too embarrassed to face these lovely people whose house I had literally just shit all over.

SALMONELLA

There are cases in which the only way to explain your actions is by having others share in your circumstances. In short, by creating forcible empathy. Diarrhea, explosive diarrhea, and painful diarrhea are all symptoms of salmonella poisoning. I'll just leave that there and you can do with it what you want.

1 whole chicken, aged unrefrigerated for 14 days
6 eggs

Let the whole chicken sit unrefrigerated for approximately 14 days, or until acrid, whichever comes first. Marinate the chicken in six whole eggs, and place it next to an old-timey radiator for at least six hours. Serve immediately.

MR. WHO

We had been dating for six months. On the Wednesday of the second week of our relationship, I realized that we had very little chemistry, and that it was time to end things before they started to get too serious. Then on Thursday of that week, her father died.

I didn't even know she had a father; I mean, I assumed since asexual reproduction didn't come into vogue until the late 1990s, but we hadn't talked about our respective parents yet. It didn't matter. Early in the morning on Thursday, there was a knock at my door. My dorm room was a concrete box with cinderblock walls that were painted off-white. Without moving from my bed, I yelled for whomever was knocking to come in. The girl I had been dating for twelve and a half days crawled into bed with me, which I thought was going to turn porn-y (I was wrong), and told me that her dad was dead.

"This is just so much easier because you're here." She kept saying that. I was planning on breaking up with her that day. I wasn't even planning on doing it in person; we had only hung out twice. I was just going to have the phone company call her and tell her.

She presented no proof that her father was dead, no death certificate or gruesome photos, but her tears sounded somewhat sincere, so I didn't break up with her. I couldn't; she was heartbroken, and scared, and while I'm a terrible person I'm not *that* terrible, plus I secretly thought that the situation could still turn to sex since we were already in bed and it would be a shame to waste a perfectly good erection.

Six months had passed and we were still dating. I had tried breaking up with her dozens of times, and each time she would bring up her dead dad and remind me that I'm the reason she's able to cope with her grief. I couldn't go through with it; that would just be bad for my brand. For the rest of my life, I'd be the guy who broke up with the grieving girl whose father just died. It would be my scarlet letter that I'd have to wear like some sort of Jew, or adulterer, or whatever it is; I never finished that book.

We grew further and further apart. We stopped having sex entirely; it was clear that I represented some connection to her dead father, and for some reason that was a turn-on to neither of us. I knew I couldn't break up with her, but I couldn't be with her, either.

My dorm room overlooked a large grassy area where students would smoke weed, play Frisbee, and commit light-to-medium loitering. I was eating an apple. It was a Red Delicious that wasn't, so I threw it from my window in the direction of some students playing Hacky Sack. As the apple struck a student wearing overalls (from a fashion standpoint, he deserved it), it hit me. I needed to fake amnesia. I wouldn't have to break up with her, but I could also make sure I never see her again; it was perfect.

That night she called my cell phone and I picked it up, inflecting upward in my greeting to indicate a vague and general sense of confusion. I explained that I had been in an accident, the details of which I didn't remember, obviously, and the doctors had told me I had amnesia. An hour later, she appeared at my door. I wouldn't let her in. I told her, "I'm not about to let a stranger into my room, and if you don't leave I'm going to have to find an adult." That angered her. Or maybe it was me calling the police and her getting arrested on domestic battery charges because she refused to leave my dorm room that angered her. I can never remember; I had amnesia.

COCONUT MACAROONS

American treasure George L. Costanza said it best: "It's not a lie, if you believe it." When lying, a dish that reinforces your lie is a subliminal and delicious way to manipulate others. According to common sense and a childhood of being forced to watch syndicated reruns of the Three Stooges, falling coconuts cause 68 percent of the world's reported concussions. Make sure to bring this up when serving the dish, because plausible deniability is the liar's currency.

⅔ cup all-purpose flour
5½ cups flaked coconut
¼ teaspoon salt
1 (14-ounce) can sweetened condensed milk
2 teaspoons vanilla extract
½ teaspoon almond extract

Preheat your oven to 350°F and line cookie sheets with parchment paper or aluminum foil. In a large bowl, stir together the flour, coconut, and salt. Stir in the sweetened condensed milk and vanilla and almond extracts. Using your hands (or a servant's hands), mix until well blended. Use an ice cream scoop to drop the dough onto the cookie sheets. Bake for 12 to 15 minutes, until the coconut is slightly browned.

CHAPTER 4

Intercourse

HEY, BABY

I don't ever want to have kids, but if I accidentally have a couple, or change my mind, one thing is absolutely for sure: No man between the ages of thirteen and eighty-five will be babysitting them. Men of this wide age range have one thing in common: They will drop anything, even their or a stranger's child, if they believe it will help them achieve coitus.

When I returned home from my freshman year of college for a month-long winter break, I received a call from my parents' neighbors with an urgent request; their regular sitter was sick with the flu, likely due to her weak, old lady immune system, so they asked me to fill in for a night. And I should mention, these were the neighbors who bought a modest house, then tripled it in size with a series of costly, yet tasteful additions. Despite my lack of childcare experience, or my general distaste for babies, I felt that this very wealthy couple needed me, and I needed some of their money, so I accepted.

After roughly thirty minutes of pretending to pay attention to their long lists of things I needed to know about their child, they finally left. Babysitting seemed easy. Primetime television, soda, and those sandwich crackers with artificial peanut butter that always manage to get stuck in your molars; I could make a career of this. But then the baby started crying. No problem, I just got a full thirty-minute orientation of how to care for children. My mind went blank, and I regretted compiling a mental checklist of food to eat from their fridge and humming the Benny Hill theme music while I should have been paying attention. I couldn't even remember the child's name, if that is any window into how little I paid attention, but no matter. I was a smart guy; I could figure this out.

As it turns out, I couldn't figure it out. The baby cried and didn't stop, which was extremely annoying, because a certain red-haired girl who was reputed for being quite un-prude had called in hopes of making plans that evening. The redhead, while a good lover, was a terrible driver, so she had failed her licensing exam four times before giving up and becoming a burden to every friend and family member she remained close to. Despite my assurance that my neighbors' house "wasn't that long of a walk" for her, she insisted that I come to her place, and before her mother gets home in about an hour. I did what any responsible man aged thirteen to eighty-five would do; I put that crying kid in my lap and drove, very cautiously mind you, to the redhead's house.

This is a family book, so I won't detail what went on at the redhead's house; however, I will say this: Bro. Nice. Toward the tail end of what may or may not have happened (it totally happened, nice!), the baby finally stopped crying. This, at the time, was a wonderful relief; however, approximately ten seconds later, it was less wonderful. As I would soon learn, the baby had stopped crying because the redhead's mother came home, saw a crying baby, and her maternal instinct did something to make it stop crying. Then she opened her daughter's door to inquire as to why there was a crying baby in her home, and discovered her daughter and a sly, handsome young suitor engaged in an unmentionable activity (cha-ching!). Worse than that was assuring her mother that the baby wasn't my and her daughter's love child that we've been keeping a secret; it's just some kid whose name I can't remember, or may have never known, that I'm currently babysitting.

As it turns out, not knowing that child's name was quite beneficial, as the redhead's mother had nobody to report me to (other than the cops, but snitches get stitches and she knew that). Her mother was irrationally prejudiced against me for some reason, but I took a liking to the redhead. After all, I was home for a month, and a month-long sure thing? You don't argue with that. It was decided I'd cook them dinner so she could get to know the real me, and again, this is a family book, but bro, month-long nice!

VEAL OSSO BUCO

They say the punishment should fit the crime, and the same goes for menu planning, so when you do terrible person things and babies are involved, you can't go wrong with veal.

½ cup olive oil
4 pieces center-cut veal osso buco
Salt and freshly ground black pepper
½ cup all-purpose flour
1 medium onion, minced
1 medium leek, minced
2 carrots, diced
2 celery stalks, diced
1 cup dry Sauvignon Blanc
4 whole fresh sage leaves
2 sprigs fresh rosemary
1 dried bay leaf
3 tablespoons fresh flat-leaf parsley, chopped, divided
2 cups peeled and crushed plum tomatoes
1 cup veal stock
1 teaspoon lemon zest, finely grated

VEAL OSSO BUCO (Continued)

Preheat the oven to 350°F. In a Dutch oven over high heat, warm the olive oil until it just starts to smoke. Season the osso buco with plenty of salt and pepper, then dredge, which is a fancy word for "coat" (no, not the one you wear), in the flour. Sear the veal in the hot oil until a delicious, brown crust has formed, then remove from the Dutch oven and set aside. Add the onion, leek, carrots, and celery to the oil in the Dutch oven and sauté for about 4 minutes. These vegetables are like irresponsible children, so do not leave them unattended for too long, or else disaster. Add the veal back in the pan, then add the wine, sage, rosemary, bay leaf, 2 tablespoons of parsley, tomatoes, and stock, and boil it all up. Cover the pot and put it in the oven you didn't forget to preheat, and braise for about 2 hours, or until your house smells like heaven (unless you're a calf). Remove the veal from the pot and reduce the sauce on the stovetop. Stir the lemon zest and the remaining chopped parsley together, and voilà, you made a gremolata, which is as fancy-sounding as it is easy. Sauce the osso buco, top with gremolata, and consider getting a vasectomy or girl vasectomy, if those exist.

THE BLOOD OF BATTLE

When I was in college, I played on an intramural flag-football team that was played with the aggression and intensity of the NFL, with the average athleticism of the AARP. In the eight-game season, my team logged a total of fourteen fights during games (team name: The Diarrhea of Anne Frank). The league was a fertile breeding ground for assholes with failed dreams of playing pro football, who instead took out their disappointment and self-loathing on their opponents. And while the league was a lot of fun in many regards, easily avoided injuries were plentiful.

During a kickoff return, I was sprinting up the sideline with only one man to beat until pay dirt. That man decided to forgo the formality of grabbing my flag and instead tackled me, sending me sliding across the artificial turf. As is customary in the game of flag football, I stood up and punched him right in the mouth, knocking his front tooth clean out and breaking my index finger. A fight ensued, the details of which I won't bore you with, but the result was two-fold: A very beautiful girl with clear daddy issues that result in her being turned on by physical violence approached me after the game, and three days later, my knee was a bloody, scabbed-over mess.

The very beautiful girl called me late one evening and asked me to come to her dorm room. She commanded me to verbally abuse her ("You don't keep your living quarters adequately clean" is all I could muster), spank her, and then once I was properly traumatized, engage in coitus with her. And at some point after the unquestionably creepiest sex I've ever had in my life, the archipelago of scabs on my knee came loose, causing her sheets to look like a *Law & Order* prop.

We awoke the next morning and discovered the mess. "Oh my God, I'm so embarrassed." She did appear embarrassed. Clearly she thought that the blood came from her, shall we say, Virginia. She ran to the bathroom, slamming the door closed. Now I knew that the blood had come from my knee, but the alternate theory to the crime was a lot easier, so I cried out in disgust, told her she must have an "angry vagina," and left.

I didn't hear from her for a few weeks; it must have been the humiliation of thinking her vagina went all Carrie on the bed. But apparently being ignored is like foreplay for girls with personality disorders. She wanted to have more traumatizing sex, assuring me that she wouldn't bleed this time. And reluctantly, I agreed. Again, she wanted spankings. For me to tell her that she was a bad girl. She begged for me to insult and humiliate her, so I said the one thing I could think of: "Your vagina didn't bleed in your bed, it was just a scab on my knee." I think she came. What can I say, women are complex.

KALE SALAD WITH CURRANTS AND CHICKEN CRACKLING

Kale is very high in vitamin K, which helps with blood clotting. It's also very en vogue at the moment because of white people, so win-win.

2 tablespoons dried currants
6 tablespoons white balsamic vinegar, divided
1 tablespoon rice wine vinegar
1 tablespoon honey
1 tablespoon extra-virgin olive oil
Salt and pepper
1 pound Tuscan kale, center ribs and stems removed, chiffonade
2 tablespoons pine nuts, toasted
Chicken skin
Parmesan cheese, shaved

Add currants to a small bowl with 5 tablespoons of the white balsamic vinegar. Let them soak overnight, then when you're ready to cook, drain the currants and set aside. Whisk the remaining white balsamic vinegar, rice wine vinegar, honey, oil, and a pinch of salt in a large bowl. Add the kale, soaked currants, and pine nuts, and toss your salad (ha!). To make the crackling, trim excess fat from chicken skin, season with a lot of salt and pepper, and roast in a 450°F oven for about 10 minutes, or until brown, crispy, and your house smells like a less shitty version of your house. Season the salad to taste with salt and pepper, sprinkle Parmesan cheese shavings over the salad, and top each with a crispy crackling.

BUST A RUT

Anybody who's had a sex rut knows, once you become aware of the fact that you're in one, 100 percent of your attention is focused on getting out of it. Ruts happen for many reasons; sometimes life gets too busy and sex takes a back seat, or emotionally, sex just isn't what you need right now (this applies only to women), or maybe you're just ugly.

I've been broke in New York City. It's not as fun as HBO makes you believe. At my brokest, I had to give up my apartment because I couldn't afford the rent; I got out of the lease and subletted a room above a corrugated cardboard factory in Brooklyn whose toxic fumes were obscured by the more pleasant aroma of the commercial bakery next door. The Craigslist posting for the room painstakingly emphasized that they were looking for a quiet, respectful person to share their space with, vegans preferred. The word "quiet" appeared in the posting seventeen times. The roommates consisted of a quiet law student, a quiet med student, and a mute PhD student (nerds), who felt that they needed quiet for their vast, important studies that could only be done in quiet. When I interviewed for the room, they asked me to demonstrate my typical "inside voice." I whispered and they all nodded approvingly. I got the room.

When I moved in, I was in the midst of a three-month-long sex rut. Losing my apartment wasn't helping things; a surprising number of women were totally not cool with the idea of doing it outside somewhere.

On the third night in my newly subletted room, I met some friends out for drinks. One of them had brought her friend along; she was cute, just moved to the city, and knew like, oh my God, nobody.

We hit it off and ended up being the last two of our friends at the bar. She suggested that we go back to my place and hang out. I suggested that maybe we should go to her place because my roommates really enjoy quiet, but she was one of those terrible people who move to New York without an apartment or plan and just leech off of their friends until they hate them. It didn't matter, though; I had a rut to climb out of.

I told her we'd have to be quiet. My roommates really like quiet. She asked if they were Asian and I felt myself liking her. We kissed for the first time in the cab on the way back to my new apartment. Then we got kicked out of the cab because I used my hands sexually on her and the cabby didn't like that. Finally, we arrived home, went to my bedroom, and started breaking the rut. I kept whispering for her to be quiet, but she didn't listen. She grabbed my right hand and stuffed it in her mouth. She started panting and moaning, each successive noise growing in volume. Then, she moved on to dirty talking.

So, if this is starting to sound kind of erotic, it was not. This wasn't your run-of-the-mill, heat-of-the-moment dirty talking; this felt more like the precursor to a very conclusive schizophrenia diagnosis. She just started listing nouns in no logical order. I heard desk chairs squeaking against the floor outside my room, then a knock on my door. I tried to stop intercoursing, but the girl latched on to my butt cheeks and wouldn't let me go. (See how good I am? Ladies can't get enough.) I tried to talk to the roommates, but a combination of lust, trauma-related shock, and alcohol prevented it from being a productive conversation.

After a few minutes, they stopped knocking, and a few minutes after that I was officially out of my rut. The next morning the girl left early. When I awoke, my roommates were waiting for me in the living room with adorable matching stern looks on their faces. They asked me what I was doing last night as if they really didn't know. I told them I was getting out of my rut. Their anger subsided and they nodded knowingly. Nerds.

SHRIMP AND GRITS WITH BACON AND TOMATO

Breakfast for breakfast is great. Breakfast for dinner is even greater. Breakfast for lunch is brunch and that just makes me feel uncomfortable.

1 tablespoon butter
1 tablespoon olive oil
1 large onion, finely diced
2 cloves garlic, minced
2 cups whole milk
3 cups water
1 cup grits
1½ cups grated Cheddar cheese
Salt and pepper
8 ounces bacon, chopped
20 shrimp, peeled and deveined
½ cup diced tomato
¼ cup chopped scallion

Add the butter and olive oil to a saucepan over medium heat. Add the onion and cook until soft and translucent, then add the garlic and cook for another minute. Raise the heat to high and add milk and water. Bring it all to a boil, then slowly whisk in the grits. Lower the heat to medium-low and simmer, stirring occasionally, for about 20 minutes. When it's done, add the cheese and season with salt and pepper. In a sauté pan over high heat, cook the bacon. When it's crispy, add the shrimp and cook until pink, about a minute per side. Add the tomatoes and scallions and sauté for one more minute. Season with salt and pepper and serve over the grits.

IT CAN WAIT

I lost my virginity in my friend's parents' office that also doubles as a guest bedroom. His parents had gone out of town, so he threw a party, and his other two closest friends and I got the VIP passes for the sleepover portion, too. My friend actually did make little laminated VIP passes that said VIF, for Very Important Friend, but we felt they were too queer, so we threw them out and vowed never to discuss them again.

After the party was the after party, and the after party was on the pullout sofa in the office that doubled as the guest room. I was passionately kissing a girl from the next town over whom I had been dating for three weeks. Soon, kissing turned to necking, which in turn became heavy petting. In retrospect, insisting that we actually pull out the bed was kind of a mood killer, especially when we had to go out and ask where the sheets were (if you're going to say your office doubles as a guest room, leave sheets on the pull-out bed; it's like nobody has any manners these days), but in the end it didn't matter; it was destiny.

I sensually groped her and counted to 100 in my head, because my uncle told me that "You gotta warm 'em up first." Finally we had disrobed, gathered all of the various accoutrements: a condom, a sample-sized bottle of lubrication, and a candle because I am romantic and also aroused by fire. We got into position, and after double-checking that I was in fact on the doorstep of the correct door, we started having sexual intercourse.

There was a knock on the door. We stayed quiet, hoping whoever was there would go away. We listened closely and heard pained breathing, a short, cyclic wheeze. They knocked again, and then tried the doorknob, but it was locked. "I need my inhaler." It was my friend whose parents were out of town. He was asthmatic.

There are two differing, fiercely opposed schools of thought on virginity; the first says that one has lost one's virginity at the moment of penetration, while the other says that penetration *and* ejaculation have to occur in order to officially lose one's virginity. Knowing full well of this national controversy, I was unwilling to stop having sex and risk still being a virgin after that night. He had asthma attacks every day; I had waited sixteen years for this. He could wait.

Approximately four minutes later we were finished; well, I was finished, so by default we were finished because I had not yet matured to be a generous lover. The wheezing had stopped. I opened the door, a condom still clinging to my penis (in case anybody wanted proof that I wasn't a virgin); my friend lay motionless on the ground in the hallway. I ran into the guest bedroom that doubles as an office, searching the filing cabinets with wild abandon for his inhaler. I located it and sprinted back to the hall. I put the inhaler in his mouth and pressed down on the canister; gas hissed from the chamber. I pressed it three more times, and on the last, he coughed and became conscious. He rolled onto his back and took deep, desperate breaths, unable to say anything. He was struggling to breathe; he seemed distant and removed. Suddenly, he looked at me and his head rolled back; he reached his hand toward me and I handed him his inhaler, desperately hoping it would save his life. But he didn't want the inhaler; he unfurled his fist, revealing a laminated VIF card that we had previously agreed to dispose of. He gave me a pained thumbs-up, then either had a seizure or winked and handed me the card. Still queer, bro. Still queer.

VANILLA-SUGAR RIMMED INHALER

Replacing a loved one's necessary medicines with more fun drugs is a great way to show him that you care. For inhalers, I like to replace the medicine with CO_2 so that they can surreptitiously take whippets wherever they are, and a festive vanilla sugar rimming not only sounds like assplay, but it tastes delicious, too.

1 vanilla bean, seeds scraped from the pod
2 cups granulated sugar
1 tablespoon fresh lemon juice
CO_2 cartridges

Slice the vanilla bean down the middle and use the blunt side of a knife to scrape the seeds away from the pod. Add the seeds and pod into an airtight container with the sugar. Let sit for at least 1 week. Replace the medicine cartridge with CO_2 somehow—be crafty. Dip the inhaler's mouthpiece in the lemon juice, then in the vanilla sugar, and enjoy!

"WHAT'S MY NAME?" IS DEFINITIVELY NOT A RHETORICAL QUESTION

I'm a real old-fashioned romantic. When I take a girl out, I'll hold the door for her, pay for everything, and won't sleep with her on the first date; I draw the line at heavy petting and/or blowjobs. This is mostly because I'm terrible with names. I never forget a face though (never, so don't try anything), but I've had both professional and personal relationships with people for years without ever knowing their name.

If you intercourse someone, it's almost essential to know that person's name. If you don't, you could call someone the wrong name, which usually results in the cessation of intercourse, often abruptly and without any regard for your feelings. This is why I tend to avoid one-night stands. I know that I'm emotionally ready to sleep with someone when I can confidently remember her name (or their names, three-somes, whoo!).

It was 3:00 A.M. and I was drunk. I appeared competent at sitting on a barstool, but beyond that I was useless. I didn't want to drink more, but cocktails kept appearing in front of me, and my arms and mouth achieved sentient thought and kept pouring them down my throat. A young lady struck up a conversation with me. I'm sure she probably introduced herself in addition to other words she probably said; however, I didn't hear any of them. This woman was into the strong, silent, and might currently be having a stroke type because after an unknown period of time I was no longer sitting on a barstool, but rather inside her apartment and she was taking my pants off. I was later told we achieved coitus with one another.

The next morning, I awoke with my mouth feeling like a small woodland creature had messily died from fear inside of it. My stirring had woken my romantic partner from the bar or tavern or family restaurant, I can't remember. She asked me if I had a nice time the evening prior. I told her, "Who's to say?" which she misinterpreted for me being deep. She kept going on and on about how she felt a very real connection between the two of us, how nobody has ever listened so intently to her, and how she's usually against one-night stands but this just felt different; this felt right.

I told her I had to go and I started to get out of bed, but she grabbed me and rolled on top of me. She was very aggressive, sexually. I tried to say no and explain that I had to go to a bris, and then I had to explain what a bris is, which kind of killed the mood for a minute, but she ensnared me. We began intercoursing and she started yelling my name with impassioned screams. Then, she asked me to say her name. I was hoping this was more of a rhetorical request said in the throes of passion, so I stayed quiet. She continued requesting it, which soon turned to demands, which felt a bit vain if I'm being honest. She wouldn't relent, so I yelled, "Maria," which is the most common female name in the world, and thereby a very good guess. But that wasn't her name, I don't think.

When she realized I didn't know her name, she got very, very preachy. The same woman who the night prior had no problem seducing and intercoursing a man so intoxicated that he wouldn't have been able to pass a dentistry exam, which are notoriously easy, had the gall to stop intercoursing in the middle of intercourse just because I didn't currently know her name. I told her that she was holding me to an unfair standard and she became even angrier. "We work together, you asshole," she said. Oh holy shit, it was the receptionist from work. Maybe I do forget faces.

BLOODY MARY

Getting blue balls is like punishing your body for what you couldn't finish. And while this won't cure blue balls (only vigorous masturbating can cure that), it will turn that hangover you have into good old-fashioned being drunk again.

Celery salt
1 lemon wedge
1 lime wedge
2 ounces vodka
4 ounces tomato juice
3 dashes Tabasco sauce
2 teaspoons prepared horseradish
2 dashes Worcestershire sauce
Pinch celery salt
Pinch ground black pepper
Pinch smoked paprika
1 slice bacon, crispy and delicious

Pour some celery salt onto a plate. Rub the pulp of the lemon wedge on the lip of a pint glass then coat the rim with the salt and fill the glass with ice. In a cocktail shaker, add the lemon and lime wedges, squeezing the juice into the shaker before dropping them in. Add everything else besides the bacon, fill the shaker with ice, and shake. Strain into the prepared glass, top it with a slice of crispy, delicious bacon, and feel better.

CHAPTER 5

Education

ASIANS AREN'T ALL GOOD AT MATH UNLESS YOU'RE A RACIST

Stereotypes are generalizations cleverly disguised as fact. Like, many black girls be tripping, but not *all* black girls be tripping. Some people find stereotypes offensive because it shows a narrow mind and an unwillingness to learn about others. And while we can all agree that stereotypes are "bad," there's also some little, maybe big bit of truth to them; otherwise, they wouldn't become stereotypes in the first place. And those truths can help you relate to people with backgrounds different than yours. For example, if you see a Native American, you know to say "How!" and to offer some firewater, their native drink. Without stereotypes, you wouldn't know that and would look like a fool, saying things like "Hello" and "Good day," which of course they wouldn't understand.

Relying on stereotypes is a dangerous game, like Mousetrap, or hide-and-seek in Uganda, and can result in embarrassing moments and huge letdowns. During my senior year of high school, the math teacher had a tradition of honoring academic achievement by hanging the name of the student with the highest test score on each test above the blackboard. And up until the last test of the year, my name was the only one displayed. Thirteen 8½" × 11" pieces of paper reading "Zach Golden," reminding every other student in that class who was running shit. And that's not meant to be braggy; however, it is super impressive so go ahead and bask in it for a moment. With one test remaining my streak was in danger, due mostly to the fact that I had already been accepted to college (the admissions office must have heard about my mathematic achievements) and thus was high or drunk approximately 100 percent of the time.

It was test day and I was woefully unprepared. I didn't even know what the test was covering; however, I was pretty sure it was math. But, being the thirteen-time test champion had its perks. While everyone else was beholden to a seating chart, I had free reign and could claim any empty seat for my own. I surveyed the room, performing an ad hoc pro-con evaluation of each open seat before choosing the seat directly behind John Park, who was either Asian or had some sort of eye problem.

I'll be frank; I cheated. And I chose John Park because I thought he'd be good at math. Because he's Asian. And Asians are good at math, apparently according to a guy who's definitely not me.

The next day I walked into the classroom, surveying the open chairs for my choice of seat, as was my prerogative. And as I settled into a chair toward the back of the classroom, my teacher cleared her throat and said, "In your assigned seat please, Zach." I searched for my name above the blackboard, but there was a new piece of paper, one bearing the name of not me. The teacher passed out the graded tests and I had scored a 71.

After class, I found John Park and confronted him: "You fucked me, John Park." I flipped him around and pantomimed sodomy. "You're supposed to be good at math."

"Why?" he asked.

"Because you're Asian, obviously."

"That's a racist stereotype," he said.

"No it's not, it's a compliment, what are you retarded or something?" As it turned out, he was some sort of retarded, at least in math. And he looked upset, like he knew he was *supposed* to be good at math, but wasn't, so that made it feel worse. And seeing how upset he was, I realized that stereotypes can be hurtful. And since I'm not a total monster, I made him dumplings because Asians like those.

PORK AND CHIVE DUMPLINGS

Pork dumplings are one of the most beloved foods in the world, and not just because there are so many damn Asians. It's because they're delicious. However, making them at home can be difficult, so stay calm, keep your wits about you, and put on Rush Hour 2 *for inspiration.*

½ pound fatty pork, ground
½ tablespoon sherry
¼ teaspoon sesame oil
½ teaspoon Vietnamese chili-garlic sauce
1½ teaspoons ginger, grated
½ teaspoon rice vinegar
2 teaspoons soy sauce

½ teaspoon salt
Pinch of white pepper
3 tablespoons cilantro stems, finely chopped
3 tablespoons chives, finely chopped
30 round dumpling wrappers
Water

Combine everything but the dumpling wrappers and water in a large bowl and stir together. Keep the bowl cold by resting it in a larger bowl filled with ice. To make the dumplings, place a rounded teaspoon of the filling in the middle of a dumpling wrapper. Moisten the area around the filling with water, then fold in half to form a crescent shape, and press the edges to seal it up. Moisten one corner of the dumpling wrapper with water, then bring the corners together to form a circular shape, pinching the corners together to get them to stick. Cook the dumplings in a large pot of simmering water for about 3 minutes and then enjoy.

THE MYSTERIOUS MIKE HUNT

When I was in high school, I didn't have very much school spirit. We were the Barons, represented by the top hat, cane, and folded white gloves in our logo. I went to school the bare minimum amount. If I had missed even a day more, it would have invalidated my entire education and I wouldn't have been able to graduate and my life would be in shambles, so I guess you could say I had it pretty figured out.

I didn't like my high school. I didn't like the building, the staff, the students, the administration, the strict adherence to only PepsiCo products even when my market analysis conclusively showed that 61 percent of respondents were in favor of becoming a Coke school. And because I didn't like the school, I felt it was my American duty to be as difficult as possible whenever possible to whomever possible.

The editor of the school yearbook was not a friend. He still isn't, actually. He had lots of school spirit, an overabundance of it, even. And he took it as a personal affront that any man, woman, or child who had the privilege of calling themselves a Baron wouldn't feel the same immense pride he felt.

One morning, he went on the poorly produced morning announcements, which were telecast on a set that lacked both personality and imagination. He detailed the wide variety of school clubs that were having their photos taken for the yearbook that day. It was also announced that students could miss class for the photos. Suddenly, I felt school spirit the likes of which I've never felt before. I was not only a proud Baron; I was the proudest Baron, a fact that I would prove by appearing in every single club photo.

By 11:00 A.M., I was in photos for the Chess Club, Science Club, Mock Trial, Muslim Student Association, and the Gay/Straight Alliance. I had a full schedule ahead of me and was going strong. Before each photo was taken, they would pass a clipboard and pencil around and you would write your name so that they could list the corresponding names with faces. Knowing that the yearbook editor believed that he had the most school spirit, I posited that he wouldn't want to be outshone by a clever, dashing young Baron such as myself. So to avoid such an unnecessary petty rivalry, I used a different pseudonym for each club photo I appeared in, which, to be clear, was all of them.

In first edition copies of the 2001 Brighton High School Yearbook, the following names were printed:

- Mike Hunt
- Haywood Jablowme
- Harry Sax
- Anita Moore Seamon
- Dang-Lin Wang
- Helda Coccen-Mihan

The yearbook distributor said it was only the second complete recall of yearbooks he had seen in his twenty-seven-year career; the first also occurred at our high school, when a local jury determined that printed photos of young men changing in the locker room did in fact constitute child pornography, despite our gym teacher's fervent claim that it was art. I was blamed and sent the bill for the cost of the replacements.

They were trying to charge $120 per copy; that's a goddamn shakedown. My father stood by me in refusing to pay. He even offered to rip out the offending pages for free, but they declined. Eventually, the school district was forced to take my family to a school board arbitration hearing, where we won our case. The yearbook editor came to the hearing with a disgusting, smug smile. But I stared right in his terrible eyes as the arbitrator, a local judge, and former highly regarded yearbook editor himself, read his opinion. He said it was "a misguided prank that should have been caught by a competent yearbook staff." Sick burn, judge, sick burn.

HOAGIE/GRINDER/HERO/SUB/GYRO

If you're being forced to apologize, it's important to be as insincere as possible. If you're sincere, it cheapens real apologies, and that's not good for business. I made my adversary this hoagie, or grinder, or hero, or sub, or gyro, to remind him of all the different names I managed to get past his incompetent yearbook staff. Burn.

French loaf, split
3 slices salami
3 slices mortadella
3 slices provolone cheese
3 slices Swiss cheese
10 rings pickled banana peppers
Olive oil

Preheat your oven to 350°F. Butterfly the loaf so that it's connected on one side; layer the meats, cheeses, and peppers. Drizzle it all with olive oil and bake until warm and crispy, about 5 to 7 minutes.

BLOWJOB-RELATED SUSPENSION #3

I was suspended from school a total of thirteen times. My first official suspension was in the fourth grade when I told a girl on the bus to suck my dick, not as an actual suggestion, but as an insult that I once heard an adult say. My suspensions ran the gamut from my fist accidentally colliding with a student teacher's face to throwing my literal feces at an entire fleet of school buses (I saved up), but the last suspension was undeniably the most embarrassing.

I went to a public high school in a safe suburb. On our free periods, we were allowed to leave the school on our own volition to stretch our legs, eat lunch, or get into unspeakable trouble, whatever we felt like doing. They believed that this was a privilege, and like all totalitarian regimes, they often revoked this "privilege" as a display of power that actually reveals their true weakness. When you had your free periods revoked, they became study hall, which was basically *The Breakfast Club*, but usually closer to lunchtime.

Study hall had its regulars, the miscreants who were in a perpetual state of trouble and would sit in the same room after school for detention, but every day new people would show up, too. Normal, popular, contributing members of society would pop in for committing some minor infraction like passing notes, or sodomy. All of my free periods were relegated to study hall; I spoke out against the injustice that the administration administered daily, and for that they tried to take my freedom.

On a cloudy Thursday afternoon, study hall had six new additions; six beautiful girls in the grade below mine who fell victim to a very funny inside joke and couldn't stop laughing during a social studies class were sentenced to study hall because their teacher hated the sound of children laughing. I showed them the ropes and engaged in some light to medium flirting.

I always drew pictures in study hall. You weren't allowed to make noise, and you had to appear to be studying, so I drew pictures. And on this day I drew six pictures of myself getting a blowjob from a disproportionally busty woman (to clarify, her body was disproportionally skinny to the massive size of her hooters). I then tore each of these six pictures into small squares, and added the text: "This coupon entitles you to: 1 blowjob for Zach Golden. Redeemable only at Zach Golden." I passed out the coupons to each of the six pretty girls, winking at each one as I motioned to my groin with finger guns; three of them thought it was funny, one rolled her eyes, one tore it up and wouldn't make eye contact, and one showed it to the study hall teacher, a former prison guard from Russia or somewhere scary.

The school decided to make a big deal about it. They called my parents and each of the six girls' parents, and we all sat in the principal's office together so I could personally apologize to each and every one of them. The principal was making a spectacle of me, humiliating me to break my spirit. I gave a classic non-apology: "I'm sorry you didn't find my joke funny." My mother looked at her feet for the entire meeting; my dad had a pretty big smile on his face and appeared to be checking out one of the girls' mothers. They suspended me for three days, and I was banned from study hall and instead had to spend free periods in the principal's office. To date, two of the six vouchers have been redeemed.

BANANA PUDDING

Sometimes laughter is the best medicine, and bananas kind of look like male sex organs, so how could that not be funny?

½ cup sugar
2 tablespoons cornstarch
2¼ cups milk
5 egg yolks
2 teaspoons vanilla extract
2 tablespoons banana liqueur
½ stick butter
3 medium bananas, sliced
12 ounces vanilla wafers

In a double boiler, mix together the sugar and cornstarch, and slowly add the milk. Stir constantly until it thickens—this dish is like a small baby and shouldn't be left unattended or shaken vigorously. In a separate bowl, whisk the egg yolks and then stir in a little bit of the hot custard. Whether you knew it or not, you're tempering, so good for you. Add the egg mixture to the double boiler and cook for 2 more minutes. Remove it from heat and add the vanilla, banana liqueur, and butter. Let it all cool. In a baking dish, alternate layers of pudding, bananas, and wafers. Start with pudding and end with pudding, like all things in life.

FENDER BENDER

I like having an enemy; it keeps you on your toes. From ages five to nine, it was Addison Delfino, who was a Jehovah's Witness, which meant that nobody in our class was allowed to celebrate holidays at school or have fun because Jehovah's a fucking dick. From ages ten to thirteen, it was my sister; we used to fight like a couple of Italians. And then from ages fourteen to eighteen, it was Adam Muller, who was previously a friend, until his mother got me (and her) very high, snorted a very large line of coke in front of my virgin eyes, and then tried to Mrs. Robinson me. I was fourteen years old. I ran home like a pussy and told my parents.

Word got around town that Mrs. Muller was a miscreant, and I was a victim. It felt odd being a sympathetic character. It was changing how people thought of me. I was no longer the dashing, young hell-raiser; I was a child who had endured a traumatic event of almost getting some with a hot, older lady. It was great; I could get away with anything. People were nicer to me, and at school, teachers wouldn't discipline me because they knew I was a delicate, abused flower.

When I was fourteen, my life revolved solely around my penis and the mysterious white substance that could come out of it. I was erect approximately 72 percent of the time. I looked at pornographic magazines with the wonder and amazement of an Amazonian tribesman seeing an iPhone for the first time, one of the later models; the earlier ones weren't all that impressive. I wasn't traumatized by a hot older lady trying to seduce me; I was traumatized that I was too chicken to take her to Pleasuretown, or at the very least the suburbs of Pleasuretown. But still, I played the part of the victim.

Adam Muller didn't take kindly to me exposing his mother as a child molester. I had the public on my side, so despite hating me, he hadn't tried anything. After school on a fall day not unlike the one in which his mother attempted to molest me three years prior, I walked to my car in the school parking lot. The high school was on a busy road and getting out of the parking lot was frustrating and difficult. There was no stoplight or stop sign on the busy road; student and faculty cars would line up, and one by one would have to gun it into a small opening in oncoming traffic. It was kind of like Frogger, but less boring.

I pulled behind a brand-new BMW. In the BMW's rearview mirror, I saw a familiar, despicable set of eyes glaring at me, the son of the pedophile himself, Adam Muller. When his car was at the front of the line, he stopped. I honked, and his taillights lit up a bright white. His car sped backward, slamming into mine. He waved a middle finger out his window.

I was laughing. The joke was on him; his expensive BMW just hit my ten-year-old hatchback. It should have stopped there; I should have been satisfied that I got the last laugh, but what's the point of getting the last laugh if your enemy doesn't see and/or hear you laughing? I put my car in first gear and pushed the gas pedal to the floor. Both cars slammed forward. He pressed his brakes, but it didn't matter; I pushed him right into the intersection, where he was T-boned by a Chevy Suburban.

His car wasn't totaled, but whatever the classification right below totaled is, it was that. He was shaken up, but without even assessing the accident scene and insurance implications, he ran from his car and attacked me. When the police came to investigate the accident scene, Adam Muller tried to blame it all on me. They didn't buy it. They had heard the stories. I couldn't possibly have done anything; I was a victim.

T-BONE STEAKS WITH ONION CONFIT

I'm a sucker for themed apology meals, so not making T-bone steaks after causing a T-bone automobile collision would just feel like a wasted opportunity.

⅓ cup olive oil
3 large onions, peeled and thinly sliced
2 bay leaves
2 rosemary sprigs
⅓ cup soft brown sugar
⅓ cup dry white wine
⅓ cup red wine vinegar
2 tablespoons balsamic vinegar
4 T-bone steaks
Lots of salt
Lots of freshly ground black pepper

To make the onion confit, add the oil to a sauté pan over medium heat. Add the onions and cover the pan; cook until they start to caramelize. Add the bay leaves, rosemary, brown sugar, wine, and both vinegars. Bring everything to a boil, then simmer for 25 minutes, or until the liquid is dissolved, stirring constantly. Discard the bay leaves and rosemary sprigs. For the T-bones, season them aggressively with salt and pepper, yelling at them and calling them names. Grill them. Serve the onion confit atop the steaks and enjoy.

AU POIVRE

My mother spent twenty years working in the kind of scary part of the inner city as a social worker for poor families. Everyone's confused as to how we're related. After a coworker of hers got mugged, she began carrying a small canister of pepper spray in her purse to ward off any would-be assailants, or Hispanics; she had no tolerance for Spanish.

When I was eleven, I had been banned from riding the bus home from school. I was still allowed to ride the bus to school because there were two separate drivers, a morning driver and an afternoon driver, and only one contacted their union representative about banning me due to what they called "continuous emotional trauma." Because of this, my mother was forced to drive me home from school each day. I sat in the back because it made it feel like I had a chauffeur, and one day I found the pepper spray in her purse resting on the seat next to me. I asked her what it was for and she told me that it shot pepper, was very dangerous, and that I should never, ever touch it again. She watched me in the rearview mirror as I nodded and pretended to put the pepper spray back in her purse.

"Why couldn't I have pepper spray?" I thought. I didn't even know spices came in spray form but of course they should; it made so much sense! Pepper made so many things better: eggs, salads, meat. And sure sometimes it made cartoon characters sneeze, but it was one of the fundamental spices in cooking. To have it in spray form was simply a convenience I wasn't willing to forgo.

The next morning, I boarded the bus, nervously clutching the forbidden pepper spray sitting loosely in my pocket. I moved to the middle of the bus and found a seat with a neighbor, Andrew Percy. He was eating a bagel and cream cheese, wrapped neatly in aluminum foil. He looked down at it unemotionally and commented on its blandness. I took a bite; it was indeed not very good. It needed something, something spicy, with a little bite and vague hints of citrus. It needed pepper. I removed the pepper spray from my pocket and showed it to the neighbor. He agreed that pepper might punch up the flavor a bit, but we both surmised that a smoked paprika spray, or perhaps something with fresh herbs in it, would have been more ideal. Nevertheless, he held the bagel out in the aisle and I sprayed it.

The air in the bus was sucked out, replaced with choking and children's tears. Kids were rolling on the ground in pain, screaming nonsensically. The bus scraped against a metal guardrail, hissing and shooting sparks as it slowed. The bagel tasted like shit, too.

I was banned from ever riding the bus again and forced to give a formal apology to the bus driver, who retired after the incident. I also succeeded in getting pepper spray banned from my school district, so in many ways I was a catalyst to reform, which nobody seemed to focus on. My mother started work early each day, and my dad didn't want to "ruin my mornings carting you around," so they bought me a bike and I had to ride to school, rain or shine. Sweet punishment.

STEAK AU POIVRE

Do not use pepper spray, Mace, or Ma$e in your Steak au Poivre. That will result in burning, gastrointestinal irritation, or an increase in money thereby leading to a proportional increase in problems.

3 tablespoons black peppercorns
4 beef fillets
Salt
2 tablespoons butter
1 tablespoon canola oil
⅓ cup cognac
1 cup beef stock
½ cup heavy cream

Take your peppercorns and crush them with a heavy pan or a hammer, or whatever you typically use to crush things. Transfer the crushed pepper to a plate and roll the fillets in the pepper until evenly coated, then liberally, in favor of pro-choice, rub both sides with salt. In a large skillet over medium-high heat, get the butter and oil hot. Add the fillets and cook until browned, about 4 minutes on each side for medium-rare. Remove the fillets from the pan and let the meat rest. Add the cognac to the hot pan, add fire to burn off the alcohol, then add the stock. Cook until the sauce is reduced by half. Add the cream and stir occasionally until thick. Season the sauce with salt and pour over steaks.

CHAPTER 6

The Law

A LAWN COCK FOR THE AGES

You can tell an asshole from a regular person by the expression on his face after his transgression. A regular person will have a sheepishness, an understanding that he did something wrong, while an asshole will look as confused as a dog who woke itself up by farting. Thankfully, modern society is built around protecting people from assholes; it's why we have police officers, lawyers, and *Night Court*.

One rainy night in high school I went to a classmate's house whose parents were out of town. After I was caught urinating in his kitchen cabinets, I was asked to leave, which I felt was extremely rude and reflected poorly upon the classmate as a host. I left through the garage, where I noticed a bright red gas tank with a yellow spigot sitting next to a push lawn mower. It called out to me and I couldn't ignore it. The EZ-Pour cap made it quite EZ to pour the gasoline with control, allowing me to expertly form the perimeter of a rather large penis on his front yard. I rang the doorbell and asked the host for a light. At first he was confused, but when I promised I would leave after he gave it to me, he reluctantly agreed (he really was an appalling host). Well, of all the burning lawn penises I've ever seen, this was by far the most magnificent.

Once the fire petered out, I left and thought nothing more of it; just some good clean fun for everybody except his lawn, which had charred grass in the shape of a giant dong burned into it. Two days later, I got a call at work from my father. "You need to come home," he said.

"My shift isn't over for three hours."

"Then I'll just tell the police to come there." There was a brief silence on the line.

"They'd be okay with that?" I was surprised.

"Just get the hell home." He hung up.

When I arrived home, there was a police officer waiting for me in the living room. He asked if I had burned a giant penis in so-and-so's yard this past weekend, and I replied, "Yeah, you saw that? Pretty great, right?" I changed the subject, offering him cookies, but he refused. "Are you sure? They're homemade." He refused again, trying to change the subject back to my alleged crime.

"So you admit to it, then?" he asked.

"I'd feel a lot better if you took a cookie." He relented and had a cookie. And then another. And then a third. Finally, when he couldn't bear to eat another delicious cookie, he decided to do some actual police work and asked me why I did it.

"I'm just wondering why the focus is on me, when we're just glossing over the fact that this guy had a party with illegal drugs and alcohol being served to high-school students." Victim blaming is often a very effective way to get out of trouble.

"You know, that's a good point." It was? It was! The cop closed his notebook, took a cookie for the road, and left. And as it turned out, my classmate was not only arrested, but his parents had to sue him in order for their homeowner's insurance to cover the fire damage. Serves him right, kicking me out of his party like that for no reason other than urinating on his food and dishware; clearly he was the asshole.

CHOCOLATE CHIP COOKIES

Homemade chocolate chip cookies are a good item to always have on hand. That way, if you're traipsing around town and you do something unspeakably terrible, you can give your victim a cookie and be on your merry way, situation dealt with.

1 cup plus 2 tablespoons all-purpose flour
½ teaspoon baking soda
½ cup unsalted butter, softened
½ cup white sugar
½ cup light brown sugar
1 large egg
¼ teaspoon salt
2 teaspoons vanilla
1 cup semisweet chocolate chips

Preheat your oven to 375°F. Combine the flour and baking soda. In a mixer with a paddle attachment, cream the butter and add the sugars, one at a time. Add the egg, salt, and vanilla, and beat until combined. Slowly, sensually even, add the flour mixture until well blended, then add the chocolate chips. Spoon onto cookie sheets lined with parchment paper and bake until the edges of the cookies are brown, about 10 minutes.

HOT FUZZ

Nothing says "I care about you" more than ordering a loved one a stripper. It doesn't matter the occasion—birthday, engagement, or death of a loved one—a stripper is a tasteful way to show someone you care. But in the wide world of strippery, there are choices to be made. One doesn't simply phone up the stripper dispatch and ask for the nearest performer; a conscientious person pays attention to details, like gender, theme or character, and whether the stripper has HIV or full-blown AIDS (or you know, neither).

Cop strippers are the best; that's a fact. With cop strippers, there is always the terrifying moment of actually believing the police are at your door (quick, hide the weed). But then, something seems a little off, and it's usually because the cop looks really slutty or has a very elementary understanding of search and scizure protocols, and then the terror becomes hot, steamy, erotic pleasure.

It was the night of my best friend's bachelor party, and after much drinking it was decided that we'd hire a stripper without him knowing. I was the best man, so it was decided I would do the procurement. I wanted to get him the best, so naturally I was in the market for cop strippers. I called the number listed in the classifieds, in an ad that featured a very attractive young lady whose father left when she was four under the heading "Performers for All Occasions." I asked for two police strippers and he quoted me "$400 per hour, and no rough stuff." The price was non-negotiable, a phrase that the man on the phone kept repeating in an echoing whispery voice for some reason. I know my friend chose me as "best man," but $400 per hour is highway robbery, so I thanked the man, but politely declined. After making a few more calls, it seemed that $400 per hour with no rough stuff was the going rate around town, and unwilling to pay what I considered an inflated price for adult entertainment, I gave up.

I knew the guys were going to be disappointed, so I did the next best thing. Now, in hindsight, it would seem that the next best thing would involve a scenario in which I only hire one stripper, hire a cheaper non-cop stripper (out of the question), or just give the money I was going to spend on the stripper to the groom as a small, symbolic token of my love. But unfortunately, my mind was so enamored with a crime-fighting stripper cop tandem that I did none of those things.

Instead I called 911 and reported a noise complaint, giving our address. As I hung up the phone, it crossed my mind that this may be a bad idea. But above all else, I'm an optimist, and I figured that maybe the real cops would just feel the vibe and decide to strip, you know, on a whim.

A couple of minutes later, there was a knock on the door. All of the guys smiled knowingly; the groom peeked through the eyehole and jumped back. "Shit! It's the cops, hide the weed!" He composed himself and opened the door, and standing on his porch were two very angry-looking cops, a man and a lady.

The cops didn't decide to strip. Instead, they decided to ask questions, very sternly. And when the groom's brother-in-law decided that the sexiness wasn't transpiring quickly enough, he decided to let the groom in on the hoax. "Relax, they're strippers."

"Sir, I assure you we are not strippers."

"If you weren't strippers, I couldn't do this . . . " The groom's brother-in-law reached out and pushed the lady cop's breasts together, then to make matters worse, motorboated. Or maybe he didn't motorboat, and it was just brought on by the TASER brand Taser he was shot with. Either way, it wasn't good.

MAPLE ICE CREAM WITH BOURBON-GLAZED BACON

Adding bacon makes anything better. Some people say they are "sick of bacon" because bacon is all of a sudden en vogue. Avoid those people. They probably refer to themselves as cinephiles (or some sort of -phile, although probably not pedo because people don't just readily admit that) and are thusly terrible.

6 large egg yolks
¼ cup sugar
Pinch of salt
1 cup whole milk
2 cups heavy cream

1 cup plus 2 tablespoons maple syrup, divided
2 tablespoons brown sugar
2 teaspoons bourbon
½ pound bacon

Preheat your oven to 350°F. Whisk the egg yolks, sugar, and salt together until smooth. Transfer to a saucepan and add the milk and cream, then cook over medium heat, stirring constantly, until it comes to a simmer. Stir in 1 cup of the maple syrup, transfer to a bowl, and refrigerate until cold, about 45 minutes. For the bacon, mix together the brown sugar, 2 tablespoons of maple syrup, and the bourbon in a large bowl. Add the bacon and mix until each piece is coated, then transfer to a baking sheet lined with aluminum foil. Bake until crispy and brush with the remaining glaze however many times you feel like in the 20 minutes it takes to cook. Pour the cooled custard mixture into an ice cream maker and churn until it's ice cream. Add the chopped glazed bacon, and churn for 2 more minutes, or until incorporated.

MOCK TRIAL

Law & Government was a mandatory class for all seniors at our high school. It was considered rigorous and challenging, and was taught by a no-bullshit man with an Afro and a wild beard. The highlight of the class was the much-talked-about, very public mock trial. The teacher played the judge; twelve students made up the jury; a black kid got chosen as the defendant, which at the time didn't seem nearly as racist as it does now; I was picked as the defense lawyer; and the extremely polite, perhaps to a fault, Ranjeet Kulrabi was named the prosecutor.

My client stood accused of burgling a home while high on crack, allegedly. He was facing felony burglary in the second degree, and a bunch of trumped-up charges that added up to my client going away for a very long time.

We set to work building our case. After a few days of poring over documents and interviewing witnesses, we had nothing. A student came into our office, which doubled as the costume closet for the drama club, and handed a note to one of my underlings, then hurried out of the room. She read the note, took a breath that one could describe as bated, then tried to surreptitiously crumple and dispose of the note, which of course I caught because I was a defense attorney and had an eye for that type of thing.

I demanded to know the contents of the correspondence. "Ranjeet's parents are getting a divorce," she said. In the Indian culture, and possibly

Native American culture (I always confuse the two), divorce is very uncommon. In fact, in India (and possibly Indian Reservations), the divorce rate is less than 1 percent, so Mrs. and Mr. Kulrabi splitting up was something of a big deal. My underling appeared sympathetic, so I fired her. She said, "Good, I wanted to be on Ranjeet's team, anyway." See, what did I tell you? I had good instincts.

Once I found out that Ranjeet Kulrabi's parents were getting divorced, we halted preparation on the case. Instead of researching, interviewing, and participating in the legal process, we got high and played dress-up with the drama club's fabulous outfits.

On the day of the trial, we gave our opening remarks, then Ranjeet called his first witness. The following is the court record of my cross-examination:

ZACH GOLDEN, ESQ.
State your name, for the record.

WITNESS
Ben Korones.

ZACH GOLDEN, ESQ.
Mr. Korones, you testified that the defendant confided in you that he committed the heinous crimes he's accused of, is that right?

WITNESS
Yes.

ZACH GOLDEN, ESQ.

Yes, what?

WITNESS

Yes, sir?

ZACH GOLDEN, ESQ.

Fantastic. Well, since you seem to be up on the latest gossip, have you heard anything about a local prosecutor's parents getting a very messy, contentious divorce?

(PAUSE)

JUDGE

The witness is ordered to answer.

WITNESS

Yes. I mean, yes, sir.

ZACH GOLDEN, ESQ.

And is this person sitting in the courtroom today?

WITNESS

Yes, sir.

ZACH GOLDEN, ESQ.

Let the record reflect, the witness pointed to Prosecutor Kulrabi. Let the record also reflect that it is unclear as to whether the divorce is Prosecutor Kulrabi's fault, but we'll err on the side of totally his fault. The defense rests.

As it turns out, we won our case. Well, we didn't win our case, but it was declared a mistrial because the prosecutor resigned, and because the prosecutor's parents decided to raise a stink with the school, which unequivocally canceled the mock trial portion of the Law & Government class in order to avoid a messy and at times nasty lawsuit. Either way, my client got justice, and we all learned a valuable lesson: You can't teach instincts.

SPICED CAULIFLOWER AND POTATOES

When you cause a divorce or at the very least contribute to it, it's considered proper behavior to cook those people a taste of their home since it will likely be the last taste of home they ever have, ever.

1 head cauliflower, cut into ¾" florets

2 large Yukon gold potatoes, peeled and cut into ½" cubes

5 tablespoons canola oil, divided

½ teaspoon cumin seeds

1 teaspoon salt, divided

1 onion, diced

2 garlic cloves, minced

2 teaspoons jalapeño, minced

2 teaspoons fresh ginger, peeled and minced

1 teaspoon ground cumin

½ teaspoon ground coriander

¼ teaspoon turmeric powder

¼ teaspoon cayenne pepper

½ cup water

Preheat your oven to 475°F. Toss the cauliflower and potatoes together with 3 tablespoons of oil, the cumin seeds, and ½ teaspoon salt. Add the mixture to a baking pan and roast for 20 minutes. In a large sauté pan over medium heat, cook the onion, garlic, jalapeño, and ginger in 2 tablespoons of oil, stirring frequently until soft and caramelized, about 10 minutes. Add the ground cumin, coriander, turmeric, cayenne, and remaining ½ teaspoon of salt and cook for 2 more minutes. Stir in the water, scraping up any brown bits from the bottom of the skillet, then stir in the roasted vegetables. Cook for 5 more minutes, or until your neighbors complain because, man, this stuff smells.

THIS IS JIHAD

I lived in an apartment on the same floor as a Muslim man. I know; I was scared, too, but don't worry, nothing bad happened to me. We got off on the wrong foot; shortly after I moved in, we were riding in the elevator with my dog, who innocently tried to smell the neighbor like a precious, little angel. He was carrying his mail, and he rolled up a magazine and struck my dog across the snout, yelling a thickly accented, "Bad dog!" My dog whimpered and darted behind my legs in fear. I love my dog. I have many, many relatives I'd sacrifice in favor of him. He is truly my best friend, and this neighbor of mine just struck him with some sort of wholesale mail-order pashmina catalog.

I always carry a knife, a fancy little wooden pocketknife with a 3½" blade that I keep plenty sharp. I carry it not for protection, but because it's proven to be handy and practical, especially when cutting through Amazon's packing tape, which must be made with carbyne and diamonds, and can you believe how wasteful they are with packing materials? My God, it's disgusting. I'm going to write them a letter. I removed the knife from my pocket, making direct eye contact with the neighbor. I slowly unhinged the blade and stared him down, squinting to show that I was serious (or Asian). "If you ever touch my dog again, I'll kill you and make it look like an accident." The elevator reached our floor and he ran into his apartment, lacking the common courtesy to wish me a good evening. I was beginning to think that Middle America was right; mighty rude people those Muslins.

For a full year, things were fine. He respected my space; I respected his. But a week after I had renewed my lease for another year, we had our second incident. A friend and her dog had come over for a doggie playdate and also hopefully sexual intercourse (between us, not the dogs). She had ridden up in the elevator with my neighbor, who apparently had rage problems when confined in vertically moving boxes because her dog sniffed the man and once again he smacked it across the snout with a rolled-up magazine.

She was visibly upset, which was really impairing my ability to get some. I asked her if she'd feel better if he apologized, and she sat up straight and said she would. I pounded on my neighbor's door so we could have a civil discussion, but he refused to open it. Knowing that if I didn't improve the mood of my dog's friend's owner, both the doggie playdate and my chance at intercoursing were going to be over, I went back to my apartment and called the Federal Bureau of Investigation and reported that my, ahem, *Muslim* neighbor has been engaging in very suspicious activity, and my God, can you believe the food they eat? It stinks up the whole floor to high heaven. The FBI person on the phone was very polite and seemed extremely interested in what I had to say.

The next day, a few men in black suits paid my neighbor a visit. He was forcibly removed from his apartment and I haven't seen him since; it's been six years, and can you believe it, they've raised the rent every year. A few months after the neighbor disappeared and his family flew in to clean out his apartment, they said he was in Cuba or something. Sounds nice; I'm glad it all worked out for him.

MENEMEN

If you're attempting to make a dish that shows someone that you understand and accept his culture, make sure it's from the correct culture. Menemen is a dish from Turkey, so make sure you don't make it for an Iraqi, Armenian, or Pilgrim and then expect that person to be impressed.

2 tablespoons olive oil
2 onions, sliced
1 red pepper, sliced
1 red chili, seeds removed, sliced
1¾ cups canned chopped tomatoes
1 tablespoon superfine sugar
4 eggs
6 tablespoons Greek yogurt
2 garlic cloves, minced
8 mint leaves, chiffonade
Salt and pepper
1 small bunch parsley, chopped

Heat the oil in a cast-iron pan. Add the onions, pepper, and chili and sauté until they caramelize and soften. Add the tomatoes and sugar, and simmer until the liquid has evaporated. Make 4 pockets in the tomato mixture and crack an egg into each of them. Cover the pan and cook for 1 minute more. Mix the yogurt with the garlic and mint leaves, then season with salt and pepper. Sprinkle the Menemen with chopped parsley and serve with a dollop of the yogurt.

DIVORCE, ALMOST

When parents get divorced, it's very important to let the children know that it's not their fault. Had my parents gotten divorced, however, it would most assuredly have been my fault. As a child, I was almost always in trouble. With regularity, I got suspended from school, kicked out of summer camps (including the one my parents directed, twice), was in trouble with the law, and frequently wore white after Labor Day just to get a rise out of people. My parents had two very different parenting philosophies; my mother believed that I needed to be controlled and constantly monitored, like some sort of Arab, while my father believed that if I died or got sent to prison, there'd be a lesson in there for me somewhere. Needless to say, they didn't see eye to eye, and not just because of their height difference.

I was not allowed to hang out with Randy. My mother forbade it. His parents owned a small business and were never home; thusly unspeakable atrocities were committed on his property with regularity. On a crisp Saturday afternoon, I was invited over to his house, but predictably, my mother said no. My father, however, unaware that my mother had already exercised her veto power, said, "Sure, why not?" and drove me over. When I arrived, my friend was sitting in his living room with twenty homemade firecrackers, which is a really nice way of saying "small, impromptu bomb," neatly laid out in a grid on the stained beige carpet.

We went outside and he lit a firecracker. After a few seconds the fuse fizzled out and nothing happened. He lit another with the same result. Finally, after trying three more, I ran to his garage and grabbed a red metal gas can that was sitting next to the lawn mower. I poured a liberal amount of gasoline on the five discarded homemade firecrackers and my friend lit them with a match. There was lots of smoke, and the flames jumped high, tickling the lowest branches of the tree overhead, but there were no homemade explosions. We poured more gasoline, and tried more firecrackers, but we weren't able to achieve satisfaction.

Dejected, we put the other fifteen firecrackers in his little brother's sandbox, emptied the remaining gasoline from the can, and tossed a match on the pile like Keyser Söze. Flames erupted upward, spewing black smoke and catching the tree that hung lazily over his backyard on fire. From the bushes adjacent to his garage, we heard loud rustling. Three police officers emerged from the bushes, yelling things like "Freeze" and "On the ground," which felt contradictory and reflected poorly upon their training. We neglected to consider that Randy lived directly behind a police station, which was convenient considering how often they came to his house.

We stood back from the sandbox, our hands in the air. I'm not a religious man, but at that moment, I prayed, "Please don't let one of the firecrackers explode." I kept repeating that to whichever God Jews are supposed to believe in; I think it's Vishnu or something. The cops had their guns pointed at us, and I figured a homemade firecracker exploding at their feet may very well result in me or Randy becoming the latest in the all-too-common "accidental" police shooting deaths. Thankfully, my friend lacked proficiency in the basic concepts of explosives construction and an accident was averted. The cops called my parents (dicks) to inform them of what I had done, and ten minutes later my father arrived. He didn't yell, punish me, or even tell me I did something wrong; he just told me that if my mom ever found out about this, they would get a divorce and it would be my fault, then we went and got ice cream because any occasion is the right occasion for ice cream.

ROAST CHICKEN

A roast chicken is the most romantic, sexiest thing you can cook to make the person you love most in the world forget, if even temporarily, that you are a horrible person. Use caution when making this for your parents, as it may result in walking in on an impromptu night-wrestle.

A chicken
½ cup unsalted butter, divided
2 teaspoons fresh parsley, chiffonade
2 teaspoons fresh thyme, chiffonade
2 teaspoons fresh rosemary, chiffonade
Salt and pepper
1 lemon, halved

Preheat your oven to 400°F. Rinse your chicken with cold water, remove the giblets, and pat it dry. Starting at the neck, stuff half of the butter, cut into thin pats, under the skin of the bird. Melt the rest of the butter and brush it on the chicken, then sprinkle it with herbs. Season with a lot of salt and pepper, and stuff the cavity with the lemon. Cook the chicken in a roasting pan until a thermometer reads 160°F. Let the bird sit for at least 5 minutes, then, and only then, may you eat it.

CHAPTER 7

Special Occasions

TOASTED

My sister and I have had a bit of a rocky road, relationship-wise. She claims to feel embarrassed by me, which doesn't seem likely, and I get mad at her for feeling that way since I fancy myself quite the gentleman; it's really a vicious cycle. So it was a pleasant surprise when her fiancé asked me to be one of his groomsmen, and on top of that, being the "witty" (she used air quotes) comedy writer of the family, I was asked to give a speech at the wedding. My parents were elated: Three decades of Hatfield vs. McCoy vs. *Predator*-type feuding between their children were finally coming to an end. My sister had decided to bestow upon me an enormous honor, to be one of the few to give a speech on arguably the most important day of her life.

Except, I didn't see it like that. I was honored—touched, even—but at the end of the day it was just a little writing gig that didn't pay. So I wrote a speech, rehearsed three-quarters of it in the mirror while I was getting ready (I was too distracted by the handsome devil looking back at me to finish it), and proceeded to get so stoned ten minutes before the ceremony that I had to interrupt the judge mid-service because it struck me as odd that everyone not in the wedding party got to sit, but we had to stand.

I figured I'd be fine for my speech because they give those at the end of weddings, and marijuana's wonderful effects only last an hour or two before you have to re-up. As we shuffled down the aisle two by two and found our table, I found myself seated next to the bride and groom.

"I'm so proud of my daughter, and so happy that she found someone as great as Josh, and I know that my pride will only grow as they continue." My father was clearly proud and slightly drunk. I thought it was weird for him to give a speech right at the beginning of the reception, but who was I to question it? I was high. "And I'm also proud . . . " God, why's he still talking? ". . . to introduce our first toast, my son, Zach."

There's nothing like a room filled with all of your extended family and also another 150 strangers all politely clapping in formal wear to make you acutely aware of how high you are. My brother-in-law nudged me; apparently I was supposed to get up, take the microphone from my father, and give a speech, not just sit in my seat with one arm raised in appreciation of the applause.

Suit makers are surely assholes. How else can you explain those stupid, impossible to access pockets on the inside of a suit jacket? It's just jerk suit makers messing with us. After removing my jacket to retrieve the speech I had stored in the interior pocket, I warmed the crowd up with a few jokes, talked about how my sister and I had always made everything a competition, and that her marrying her husband wasn't really a victory over me because I didn't have a shot at dating him. Not bad, but unfortunately assholes, much like Asian female drivers, don't stop when they're supposed to.

"God knows if I had a run at him, I'd suck his cock till the house caught on fire, then we'd see who he'd choose." That was the last line of my wedding speech. It was ad-libbed. And while it may not have been my finest moment, the cheesy "Recipes for Love" speeches that followed surely weren't as memorable, nor did they raise important questions such as "What is sucking cock?" to the children in attendance.

EGGS WITH RICOTTA AND CHIVE

Breakfast is the best meal for an apology because you have a full day to benefit from the rare positive attention that you're sure to receive. Also it's reputedly the most important meal of the day, so that has to count for something.

4 large eggs
1 tablespoon fresh chives, chopped, divided
3 tablespoons butter, divided
Salt and pepper
½ cup fresh ricotta cheese
Baguette slices
1 clove garlic, halved

Whisk the eggs and most of the chives until well blended. Melt 2 table-spoons of butter in a nonstick pan over medium heat and add the eggs. Scramble the eggs. If you think this book is going to tell you how to do that, you are wrong. Season the eggs with salt and pepper, and don't overcook them. Pull off the heat and add the ricotta, stirring until incorporated. Toast the baguette slices, rub them with garlic, butter them, and throw some of the eggs on top. Make it look real fancy with some more chives garnished on top.

SURPRISE, I GOT TOO HIGH TO LEAVE THE HOUSE, AGAIN

Assholes aren't capable of having *any* involvement in a surprise party, much less planning one themselves. In fact, it's advisable to hide the occasion from any and all assholes, so that it's a surprise not only for the guest of honor, but also for any terrible people in attendance. As an experiment, tell an asshole you know that you're throwing a surprise party for a mutual friend, and you'd like him to bring cookies. Then, wait twenty-four hours and call the aforementioned friend. With 100 percent clinical certainty, that asshole will have called the friend and asked him point-blank, "What kind of cookies do you want for your party?" Seriously, go try it; we'll wait.

I once threw my girlfriend a surprise party on her birthday. Why? I'm not sure. Probably equal parts I loved her and I wanted to see if I could keep it a secret. I couldn't. But damn it, I got sort of close.

I invited all of her friends, booked a private area in the back of her favorite restaurant, corresponded and planned on a dummy e-mail account, and threatened her friends with physical violence if they ruined the surprise. Dozens of friends were slated to attend; friends of hers were planning on flying in for the occasion. It was shaping up to be quite the shindig.

I had made it to her birthday. She kept asking what our plans were for dinner, and not wanting to be too vague as to arouse suspicion, I would say,

"Well, I don't know about you, but I'll be dining at the Y," and then would pantomime cunnilingus.

The party was set to begin at 7:00 P.M., sharp. But around 6:45 P.M., I began getting texts from her unreliable, terrible friends. They were running five minutes late, or ten minutes late, or fucking thirty minutes late (you know who you are, jerks). I had to stall. For the "surprise" to be optimally surprising, everyone needed to be there; the guest of honor is to be the last to arrive. So I did what any sensible person would do and suggested we smoke some pot before we go to dinner. She agreed, probably because she thought that I had forgotten to make dinner plans and needed to buy time. The only problem was, we got much more high than originally intended, high enough that leaving the house seemed like wayyyyyy too much to handle.

I told her every last detail of the party, and then convinced her that "now that you know it's *like* we went." Then, in a surprise twist, we both agreed to just skip it (we're now married; she's a keeper), drove (cautiously; I'm not a maniac) to Popeyes, got fried chicken and biscuits, and had a whole bunch of people to apologize to.

POT GUMMY BEARS

They say you shouldn't judge a man and/or woman until you've walked a mile in their shoes. I don't know what footwear has to do with anything, but the point is: when you do stupid things when you're high, get your victims high, too.

1½ grams cannabis oil
1 (3-ounce) box of Jell-O, any flavor you want
7 unflavored gelatin packets (7 tablespoons)
½ cup cold water

Mix all of the ingredients in a small saucepan over low heat. Stir constantly until the mixture is melted and smooth. Remove from the heat and pour into plastic candy molds. Freeze until set, about 20 minutes. Remove from the molds and, whoa man, enjoy.

BAR MITZVAH INCIDENT(S)

I was kicked out of four bar mitzvahs as a child. Well, technically three bar mitzvahs and one bat mitzvah, and also, unrelated, I was kicked out of a Jewish funeral once. And the Jews, they must be talkers because after a while, I stopped getting invited to the various mitzvahs. Word was going around the Jewish part of town that I was a bad egg, like Norman and Myra's granddaughter, you know, the one with the lip ring.

The invitations stopped coming after the third; the first two were minor infractions. The first, I got drunk because my friend's uncle kept sneaking me drinks and I vomited on the mother of the newly minted man. The second, I wasn't even technically kicked out, more "asked to leave," because I got an erection while slow dancing with a girl from school. Everyone acted like it was my fault that my dance partner had emotional issues and was probably molested at a very young age and started giving me a sobbing, over-the-pants hand job on the dance floor (you never forget your first). The third, however, hindsight tells me I probably deserved that one.

In the mid-'90s, glow sticks were all the rage. In fact, *Man Today*, the Mid-Atlantic region's leading bar mitzvah trade journal, rated glow sticks as the second-best bar mitzvah dance floor prop, right behind the popular "Kiss Me, I'm Officially a Man" novelty pins. This bar mitzvah had glow sticks that were shaped like long necklaces, which could be worn as jewelry or a funky hat, twirled about, or in the case of me, cut open by rigorously sawing the casing with plastic cutlery.

The glowing liquid oozed out and beamed a bright green on whatever it touched. It smelled like chemicals and stained mightily, but it glowed! With my previous two mitzvah-related ejections public knowledge, the bar mitzvah boy's brother, who was two years younger and very annoying for being so young, trailed me like I was some sort of Italian.

The key to shaking a tail is to not let the tail know you see him, until it's too late. So as I turned a corner, I stopped and waited. When the brother appeared seconds later, I whipped him with the cut-open glow stick necklace and yelled "night vision!" The liquid poured out, landing squarely in both eyeballs. Well, this being a bar mitzvah (and not, say, a Communion), everybody panicked and made a lot of noise, and Mom and Dad just *had* to go with their not-celebrating-his-bar-mitzvah-that-day son to the hospital. And after accusing the family of being racist for kicking me out, I realized that just an apology wasn't going to cut it; more was required of me. I needed to do this family a *mitzvah* (it means "good deed," in Jewish).

BORIC ACID EYEWASH

Food eases the pain that terrible people cause. However, sometimes there are more pragmatic ways to ease pain, such as a DIY soothing eyewash.

1 cup water, boiling
1 teaspoon boric acid powder, medicinal quality
Cotton balls

Boil 1 cup of water and add the boric acid powder. This is very important: You should only use medicinal-quality boric acid powder; there is other shit that is used to kill bugs and if you use that, then this turns into a recipe for blindness. Stir the acid powder until dissolved and let the mixture cool to lukewarm. Soak a cotton ball in the mixture, and apply to whichever eye is in need of relief. Repeat until it stops hurting, physically.

SURPRISE?

When I help with celebrations, I'm usually given tasks reserved for children like choosing which flavor of cake to buy at a bakery where chocolate and vanilla are the only two options, being in charge of confetti, or performing rectal probes to ensure that guests aren't smuggling drugs and/or contraband into the celebratory venue (children have small, agile hands). I get assigned these tasks because I have a long history and proven track record of ruining, or at the very least, making worse, the supposed happiest day of someone's life.

My mother was turning forty. My father was determined to throw her a surprise party that she'd remember for the rest of her life, or at least for a while. He enlisted the help of her family and friends, my sister, and most unfortunately, me. He invited anyone meaningful to her: her parents, sisters, generations of cousins, aunts and uncles she hadn't seen in years, friends she hadn't spoken to since college, and one woman who my mother thought was dead (she wasn't then, but now is). Everyone was to gather at her best friend's house, where a lavish party, catered by a company that was widely considered the consensus #2 best catering company in the Greater Rochester Area at the time, waited for her arrival.

My father laid out my role quite simply. "You forget that you ever knew that there was a party. I didn't mean for you to find out, and frankly, I'm more than a little worried." Easy, I could handle that. The plan was, and I only found this out by monitoring my father's phone calls, he would say he is taking my mother out for a nice dinner, and she would drop me at her best friend's house who would be babysitting me. When she went inside to drop me off and pre-emptively apologize for my behavior, they'd all yell "Surprise!" and then enjoy the second-best catered meal in all of Rochester.

My father was serious about this party; he had invested so much of himself into pulling it off, so I embraced my role. I forgot all about the party, just like he asked. I had managed to induce a highly selective amnesia that wiped my memory clean, like one of those neuralyzers in *Men in Black*, which, not to get off topic, looked a lot like erotic vibrators. So on the day of my mother's birthday, when she informed me that she was dropping me at her best friend's house while she and my father went out to dinner, I refused to go.

I hated being babysat. I was fourteen years old; it was embarrassing. And since I had obediently forgotten all about the party, just as my father had asked, I was steadfast in my desire to not be babysat. After an hour and a half of clinging to various pieces of heavy furniture and threating to call Child Protective Services, my mother got me into the car and en route to the party. And when she opened the door and 120 of her closest friends and family yelled "Surprise!" in unison, she started crying. Not tears of joy. Tears of stress and anguish, and being at her visible breaking point. My father handed her a cocktail, which she downed in one sip; he comforted her and eventually she cheered up and enjoyed herself. He pulled me into the kitchen, where the caterers were doing a bang-up job truly worthy of their #2 culinary ranking, and asked me why I had refused to come to the party. I said, "Dad, if I knew about the party, would I have acted this way?" Then I winked at him, made finger guns, elbowed him in the ribs, and walked away.

CUNNINGHAM

Alcohol is a dangerous substance that can lead to liver disease, memory loss, and even death. But, it's socially acceptable and can lead to memory loss, and sometimes you just want to forget.

1½ ounces Scotch
½ ounce fresh blood orange juice
¼ ounce fresh lemon juice
¼ ounce Bénédictine
¼ ounce Heering Cherry Liqueur

Add all of the ingredients to a shaker and fill it with ice. Shake, and strain into a chilled cocktail glass. Garnish with brandied cherries, and if you'd like to be really fancy, a flamed blood orange twist.

A GIFT FROM GOD

Religion is confusing. My friend Dan was and probably still is a malfeasant. When we were younger, he started fights wherever we went, was unmercifully mean to anyone he didn't like, which was everybody, and frequently, at the grocery store, he would use the "7 Items or Less" express checkout line despite clearly having more than seven items. In addition to being the worst person I've ever known, Dan was also a Catholic.

When we were nineteen, Dan got a girl, whose name he was not yet acquainted with, pregnant. And instead of getting an abortion, giving the baby up for adoption, or floating it down a river in a basket and hoping it would understand the similitude to Moses and would just go with it, he proposed to her and she said yes.

This guy was my friend, but I don't like him. I never have. It's a classic Elvish and Dwarvish type of relationship; we may not like each other and we both may lay claim to Rivendell, but when a bunch of orcs are trying to murder you at the behest of a dark spirit represented by an evil ocular mass, you have to band together despite your differences. He was a powerful ally, so despite hating him, when I was asked to be a groomsman I accepted.

There was only one rule at the wedding: There should be no mention of the child conceived out of holy wedlock. Neither his nor her parents knew about the child; they believed that these two strangers with nothing in common other than bad morals just fell in love really, really quickly. Nonetheless, I gave my speech (it killed) with no mention of their unborn child.

Every group of friends has a "stupid friend," and in my group it was Jeremy. He was a sweet, dumb Lenny (from *Of Mice and Men*, God, read a book) and was just plain nice. I followed Jeremy to the bathroom and, using my superior intellect, manipulated him into amending the ending of his speech. I told him that telling the whole room how "excited he was for the baby to be born in four months, because to be clear you guys are five months pregnant with a child conceived out of wedlock" would be the perfect ending, and it was. A few people cried. A few people laughed. Okay, one person laughed, it was me.

GOCHUJANG SPICY PORK RIBS

Many pregnant women crave spicy food and shit. Many pregnant women are also, and I'm generalizing here so don't jump all over me, very, very moody. This all adds up to the importance of learning some good spicy recipes when someone you know is pregnant, because her general air of moodiness means at some point you'll have something to apologize for and apparently having a human growing inside of you gives you carte blanche to be temperamental.

½ cup gochujang (Korean hot pepper paste)
2 tablespoons dark brown sugar
2 tablespoons soy sauce
2 tablespoons unseasoned rice vinegar
2 teaspoons toasted sesame oil
Salt
3 pounds pork ribs, baby back, cut into individual ribs

Whisk the gochujang, brown sugar, soy sauce, vinegar, and oil until smooth, then season with salt. Toss the ribs and half of the marinade in a baking dish. Cover the ribs and chill for at least 4 hours. Preheat your oven to 350°F. Bake the ribs, covered, until the meat is tender, about 1 hour. Uncover and increase the oven temperature to 450°F. Roast the ribs, turning them occasionally, until tender, about 45 minutes. During the last 10 minutes, brush the ribs with the reserved marinade. Let the meat rest for 5 minutes and then enjoy.

CHAPTER 8

Children

CHRISTIANS LIE TO THEIR CHILDREN

Children are so easy to manipulate because they're stupid. They have to be warned repeatedly not to get into vans with strangers promising them candy because they don't have the cognitive power to avoid living out a *Law & Order: SVU* plotline in exchange for sweets. And the worst part is, most parents do nothing to make their kids less stupid. They fill their heads with lies in order to manipulate them into doing what they want. Case in point: jolly old Saint Nick.

The day that a child discovers that Santa Claus is fake and his parents are terrible liars must also be a sad day for the parents. Now, instead of just filling their child's head with convenient, easily uncovered lies, they have to do some actual parenting and not bribe their children into being "nice."

When I was five years old, my dad sat me down to drop some knowledge. He told me about nuclear war, the mechanics of sexual intercourse, what drugs were okay to try, and which ones would ruin my life; then he let me smoke my first cigarette. After mocking me for "coughing like a pussy," he asked if I had any questions, and I had just one.

"Is Santa Claus real?"

"100 percent fake." He gave me a long-winded explanation of how Santa Claus was a commercialized obfuscation of religious ideals that was wrapped in fancy paper and sold to the masses, then offered me a sip of whiskey because "damn it, you're gonna try it someday, might as well be in a safe environment."

My kindergarten class had a "Winter Carnival" coming up. It had previously been a Christmas party, but myself and three other Jews ruined that for everyone, which the other students liked to remind us of with well-timed burns like "Thanks for ruining the Christmas party, you dumb kike." Part of the Winter Carnival was learning about all of the major religions' winter celebrations, and when we inevitably got to Santa Claus, I casually raised my hand to ask a question.

"My dad said that Santa Claus is 100 percent fake, and that Christian people lie to their children. And that pornography is just part of growing up, so don't be ashamed to look at it." It wasn't a question so much as a few statements. The wind was taken out of the room. Children were crying, pounding their fists against the ground, unable to come to terms with their reality, which up until this point was just a series of lies.

I was sent home from school, not technically suspended, but asked to leave for the day. That was nothing compared to the phone calls my father had to endure from parents who were looking forward to at least seven more years of lying to their children. He would listen to them with a calm smile as they screamed on the other end of the line. Then, when they finished their tirade, he would calmly ask, "I'm sorry, what are you selling?" He was a strong man, but I felt like I owed him an apology. Being five, I didn't know how to make a dish to appropriately say I'm sorry, so I made him the only thing he'd taught me to make: a drink.

SCOTCH ON THE ROCKS

Alcohol is probably the best way to say you're sorry because if you drink enough of it, your problems will either go away or new ones will appear, but either way you're covered.

Scotch
Ice

Pour Scotch over the ice. Stop pouring just short of the rim of the glass. Repeat.

BIRDS DO NOT MAKE SUITABLE PETS FOR ANYONE

When I'm driving I have a surefire method of never getting a ticket, while still driving fast and recklessly, and very often under the influence. Just drive normally and safely, and then when some asshole races past you, going thirty over the speed limit and weaving in and out of cars, follow him (or her, but let's be honest, him). Stay at least 500 feet behind this driver and enjoy care-free cruising because if you pass a cop but he's out in front, guess who's getting pulled over (if you guessed him, you're right and get five points). The point is, when you're an asshole, you should always have a patsy.

Parrots seem awesome, if you're from an impoverished former Soviet-bloc country that's been ravaged by war and genocide; otherwise, parrots kind of suck. But while parrots are terrible pets, they make excellent patsies.

My cousins had a parrot (it died, thank God). Its name was Henry and it spoke incessantly in unintelligible gerunds without ever bothering to ask how any else was doing. They also had a two-year-old named Maya, whose first words were "uh-oh." They had been worried that Henry and Maya wouldn't get along since Henry liked to randomly bite and claw strangers for no apparent reason other than his species is dick-ish by nature. I figured I could get Henry out of the picture if I could only exacerbate the tension between their parrot and their child.

My grandfather had died and family had flown in from around the country for the funeral and to sit shiva at my cousin's house. Henry was a much-needed bright spot, impressing everyone with his nonsensical "speech" and overall bad attitude. The bird was upstaging Maya, who was being held by my mourning grandmother. Maya changed all of that in an instant when she said her second words: "Seig heil."

The room went quiet; people speculated that it just sounded like *seig heil*; she couldn't possibly have said such nonsense. But suddenly, the bird genius Henry chirped in, "Seig heil." He said it again. "Seig heil." Then again, and again, and again. "Seig heil, seig heil, seig heil." Shiva was way more fun than I thought it would be.

I'm not a monster. I would never teach my darling baby cousin to say terrible, embarrassing things. And I didn't because I had a patsy. His name was Henry, and shortly after that incident and several others where he debuted his new vernacular of "More cock please," "OJ is innocent and she had it coming," and "Kiddie porn is the only way I can get off," he was given away to a local bird shelter, which apparently exists. And although Henry thought he was so great because he could mimic human words, he wasn't smart enough to mimic an asshole by always having a patsy. Stupid fucking bird.

DRUNKEN PARROT

Themed apologies are a risky endeavor. On the one hand, it could show how creative and thoughtful you are; on the other, it could trigger a post-traumatic stress episode that further exacerbates the problem, so give that a think, or at least half of a think.

Ice
2 ounces pineapple rum
2 ounces coconut rum
1 ounce spiced rum
½ cup freshly squeezed orange juice
½ cup pineapple juice
¼ teaspoon vanilla extract

Add ice to a blender until it's ⅔ full. Add all of the ingredients and purée until smooth. Serve in a highball glass or really whatever vessel you want; this is not a sophisticated drink.

ADOPTED

My cousin is Asian. She has been for as long as I can remember. She was adopted by my aunt and uncle in 1984, when an Asian child was considered the "must-have" item of spring fashion. At four years old, I began to notice that we looked different, her and I, so I asked my parents why that was. They explained that she was adopted, then explained what adopted meant, and then they dangled very shiny keys above my head and I got distracted; then we all got ice cream.

She was adopted; it was no secret, I thought. But it was a secret, one that my aunt and uncle had spent many late nights discussing, intricately plotting out how they would one day break the news to their "daughter."

It seemed so obvious; most children look like their parents. So when you see a little Asian girl with my aunt and uncle, who always manage to look like background actors from a community theater production of *Fiddler on the Roof*, one would think that they are either kidnappers or that she's adopted.

Our families had gotten together one weekend, and Asian cousin, two other peripheral family members, and I were playing in the backyard. We chose the game Cowboys and Indians, both for its classic, Americana charm as well as its clear lesson in white hierarchy. We were splitting up teams and my Asian cousin wanted to be a cowboy. I would hear none of this. First, it's Cow*boys* and Indians, which indicates that multiple boys must make up that team regardless of a female presence, and since her being a "cowboy" would preclude another boy from being a cowboy, we would be undercutting the integrity of the entire game. Secondly, she was (and still is) Asian, and an Asian cowboy? Yeah right, that's a good one.

She asked me what I meant by, "She's Asian." She is Jewish, she explained, which is not a nationality, but neither is Asian so who was I to split hairs? We had opened Pandora's box, which I'm actually not sure the story of, but let's assume that Pandora's box contained some sort of informational pamphlet explaining adoption.

When she realized that she was adopted, her face lost all color and she moped around like a sad *Peanuts* character. Her eyes seemed dull and heavy, and she excused herself from the game. She refused to speak to her parents. She told them point-blank, "You are not my parents. You stole me . . ." which wasn't a direct quote of something I had told her, but it was definitely an accurate paraphrasing. The anger lasted about six months, and after lots of family therapy with a local psychotherapist, the author of the critically acclaimed *Why Don't I Look Like Daddy? The Bastard Child's Guide to a New Father*, things started to get better. My aunt and uncle blamed me, but come on, guys. Asian cowboy? I'm not buying it.

THIT KHO BO

Thit Kho Bo is basically Asian beef jerky, which I associate with cowboy food and for some reason railroad heists. If you can destroy someone's dream and rebuild it and make it come true with food, then you don't even have to apologize; you can just say "You're welcome."

2 pounds beef rump or bottom sirloin roast
6–8 Thai chilies, chopped
1 large stalk lemongrass, trimmed, halved, sliced thin
⅓ cup lightly packed light brown
2½ tablespoons fish sauce
2 tablespoons light (regular) soy sauce
1 tablespoon dark (thick) soy sauce

Preheat your oven to 300°F. To make the beef easier to cut, freeze it for 45 minutes. Cut it across the grain into thin pieces, about 1/8" thick. For the marinade, put the chilies, lemongrass, and sugar in a food processor, then pulse to a fine texture. Add the fish sauce and soy sauces, and blend. Pour the marinade on the meat, mix it all up, then cover and let marinate for 1½ hours. Line two baking sheets with foil, and place drying racks on the sheet trays to elevate the beef and let it drip down onto the sheet trays. Put the beef on the racks; bake until the beef is a dark red-brown and the pieces have shrunk by 50 percent.

G.I. JOE

From a very early age, I've been quite proficient at manipulating people and small animals. When I was three, I used to walk up to strangers and ask them, "Do you have a penis or a vagina?" just to catch them off-guard and give myself the conversational upper hand, should I try taking a run at their wife or girlfriend. I could manipulate my way out of trouble with adults, but with other children, I could rule them all.

When I was four years old, I went to a particularly rough daycare center. If you went in there with the prison mentality—keep your head down but don't take shit from nobody—you'd be just fine.

On my first day, a morbidly rotund five-year-old pushed me down, took my Snake Eyes G.I. Joe figurine, then lumbered away like an Ent, only less sentient. Everyone in the daycare stopped and took notice, waiting to see how the kerfuffle would unfold. "Hey, you fat piece of shit." I was talking to the fat piece of shit that took my Snake Eyes. He kept walking away, ignoring my apropos taunt. I looked around and saw a pale, young, ginger child playing with wooden blocks. I walked over to him, pushed him over, took a block, then repeatedly struck the fat piece of shit in the back of the head with it until I saw blood and got lightheaded. After that, nobody fucked with me.

I began stealing G.I. Joes from the daycare center, perhaps as symbolism, perhaps because G.I. Joes are an all-American toy that promotes American values, and above all else, America; we'll never know. Had I been a luckier child, bequeathed with the 91-inch-long by 36-inch-wide (by 32½-inch-high) G.I. Joe's USS *Flagg* aircraft carrier, I would have had enough soldiers to confidently man the entire ship, even if a large percentage got food poisoning from some Salisbury steak that had spoiled but Roadblock served anyway. My method of theft was quite simple: seek out G.I. Joes I wanted, put them in my pocket, and leave with my bounty.

It was not part of the plan to get caught, but I did. The daycare owner had noticed a figurine sticking out of my bathing suit shorts, which for some reason I used to wear as regular shorts despite their useless mesh pockets (I also wore bike shorts, recreationally). She said she was going to have to tell my parents, who would almost assuredly not be pleased. No matter how much I tried to manipulate the owner, she wouldn't budge.

I was not going to stand for this. I walked over to a chessboard, where the young ginger lad was playing an equally weak child who I told to scram. I asked the ginger if he knew how to play chess, and he did not. I explained that the whole purpose of chess is for every other piece on the board to protect the king. Pawns die by the handful to dutifully assure the safety of their leader, same with rooks, bishops, the queen, and the horsey things. He stared at me blankly. I asked him if he knew what allegory was, and again he did not. Once I had explained allegory, he got the picture; I was the king, and it was his duty to protect me.

He marched up to the owner of the daycare center and claimed responsibility for the theft, explaining that he had threatened me and I was stealing the G.I. Joe for him out of fear. The owner reluctantly bought the story, likely due to some pretty convincing crying on his part. I thanked the ginger and punched him in the mouth, knocking out two baby teeth in the process, just in case he started believing his lie. I didn't take shit from nobody.

CARROT CAKE

If you wrong gingers, just make them carrot cake. Besides being a delicious cake that is a good source of beta-carotene, the carrots remind them of their own hair and the cream cheese frosting of their fair complexions. It just shows that you care.

2 cups all-purpose flour
1 cup white sugar
1 cup light brown sugar
2 teaspoons baking soda
2 teaspoons ground cinnamon
1 teaspoon salt
4 eggs
1½ cups vegetable oil
3 cups grated carrots
1 pound cream cheese, room temperature
1 stick salted butter, room temperature
2 cups powdered sugar
1 teaspoon vanilla extract

Preheat your oven to 350°F. Grease and flour three 9-inch round cake pans and line them with parchment paper. Combine the flour, sugars, baking soda, cinnamon, and salt. Add the eggs and vegetable oil and, using a hand mixer, blend until combined. Add the carrots, stir to incorporate, and then pour into the cake pans. Bake for about 40 minutes, then remove them from the oven and cool for 5 minutes. For the frosting, add the rest of the ingredients into a bowl and beat until fluffy using a hand mixer. Ice the cake, then enjoy.

HIDE-AND-GO-SEEK

Nobody has ever died while I'm babysitting them. And I'm proud of that because there have been some close calls. Starting at twelve years old, I babysat for my neighbors who had two kids, ages two and four, at the time. I had the job down to a science. Every single time I babysat, I forcibly demanded that we play hide-and-go-seek.

Hide-and-go-seek is unquestionably the greatest game in the rich history of family gaming. It's built upon the foundation of two magical concepts: children being silent and hidden. In fact, historically, this game was referred to by another name, "Before You Had Kids," but over the years people felt hide-and-seek rolled off the tongue a bit better. The kids would hide, and I'd tell them how amazing they were at hiding, not to build positive self-esteem, but to make them believe it is plausible that it takes me between three and six hours to find them each time we play. They would hide; I would watch television and every five to ten minutes yell, "Wow, you sure have great hiding spots!" to keep them on their toes.

In reality, these kids were terrible at hide-and-go-seek. Terrible to the point that I thought they might be severely learning disabled; typically they'd hide behind a chair with their eyes closed, loudly breathing from their mouth. After a few months of slowly shaming them for their nonchalant attitude toward hiding, they began to find new hiding spots, better hiding spots, where I wouldn't have to listen to their incessant mouth breathing and I could focus on the television and eating microwavable soft pretzels with the little rock salt packets.

One evening, four and a half hours into my "seeking," I received a phone call from their parents. They were coming home early (it was probably marital problems; he had a wandering eye) and told me that they should be home in the next fifteen minutes or so. No problem, just have to find the kids, ensure that they don't appear physically injured, and make it look like we had completed some of the educational activities their parents had left for us. I found the four-year-old with ease; he was hiding beneath the blown-in insulation in the attic, which was a hiding place that I taught him about months prior. Together, we seeked his younger sister, but we were having difficulty locating her. The living room lit up as headlights shone through the bay window facing their driveway; they were home.

I yelled the little girl's name and searched frantically, but it was too late. I greeted them and explained with a smile that I couldn't currently find their daughter because she was such a proficient hide-and-go-seek player. They seemed more worried than proud. Together, we scoured every inch of the house, each room becoming more hurried and desperate than the last. After an hour, the father called the police. The mother wept quietly in the kitchen; I tried to comfort her and convince her that maybe her daughter has a future in competitive hide-and-go-seek and this would prove to be a pivotal moment, but it was no use.

Suddenly, from the basement, we heard a loud "I found her." Which isn't technically correct; he should have yelled "Olly olly oxen free" to indicate that all players had been caught, so I corrected him. As it turns out, she was in the dryer with the door closed, asleep. That's a great hiding spot.

SOFT PRETZELS

People seem to think that breads are difficult to make, thereby making them a wonderful apology that appears sincere due to the effort. People are wrong, though, and breads are easy, so exploit this pseudo-myth for your benefit. Make sure to casually mention how "labor intensive" it was to create such an item, and try not to wink because that would ruin it.

1 cup warm water

1 (¼-ounce) envelope active dry yeast

3 cups bread flour

1 tablespoon coarse kosher salt

2 tablespoons light brown sugar

4 tablespoons unsalted butter, softened

8 cups water

½ cup baking soda

Pretzel salt

Combine the warm water and yeast in a bowl and let it stand until it foams on the surface, about 10 minutes. If mixture doesn't foam, your yeast is dead so try another envelope. In another bowl, combine the flour, salt, and light brown sugar. Add the yeast mixture and butter to the flour mixture and stir together with your hands until it forms a dough. Knead the dough on a floured surface for 8 to 10 minutes. Put the dough in a lightly oiled bowl and cover with a kitchen towel. Leave it on the counter to rise for 2 to 3 hours. When the dough has doubled in size, divide it into eight pieces. Form each piece into a pretzel—figure it out and use your imagination. Heat your oven to 450°F and oil two large baking sheets. In a stockpot, bring the water and baking soda to a boil. Add the pretzels one at a time and boil for 30 seconds, then transfer to the baking sheets. Sprinkle them on both sides with pretzel salt, then bake for 8 to 10 minutes in the oven.

CHAPTER 9

Drugs and/or Alcohol

DRUNK DRIVING

I was a just a lad when Disney released the great American film *Blank Check*, the story of a young scamp whose bike gets run over by gangsters who give him a blank check to replace it, but he writes the check for one million dollars instead of a realistic cost of bicycle replacement and lives large until the gangsters inevitably want their money back, at which point the young boy learns that there are more valuable things than money. It was after seeing that film that I began hating the rich. The film was about an irresponsible kid who blew a million dollars on stupid shit that nobody needs, not to mention the fact that the kid spends at *least* 10 million bucks, but the film's producers think we'll believe that wherever they are, U.S. currency is worth roughly thirty times the market value? Get real guys, not a chance.

When I was sixteen, a rich classmate's parents threw him a Sweet Sixteen party. It was lavish and had a fine assortment of foods from all of the continents; even Antarctica was represented with a snow cone machine, which to their credit was clever. The night was highlighted by everyone being dragged outside against their will in order to see the birthday boy's present, a brand-fucking-new Audi RS6.

It wasn't enough to give a sixteen-year-old a $120,000+ car; they had to make a show of it, to make sure everyone in attendance understood that they can wipe their ass with money if they please, which they don't because, contrary to popular belief, money chafes.

Once the spectacle was over, everyone went back inside the rented venue, and the new car was parked in the back corner of the lot with a two-space buffer on each side. I made eye contact with two of my friends and we nodded knowingly at one another, accepting our duty as terrible people to mess with that car. I stole a bottle of Scotch from the bar; my two friends gathered world cuisine to feed at least ten worldly, diverse men; and together, we locked ourselves in the bathroom, ate to capacity, and drank.

At sixteen, I had been drunk before, but never like this. The three of us polished off a bottle of Scotch (single malt; we had standards) and stumbled out of the bathroom. My head felt heavy, and my limbs worked like I had been wheelchair-bound for years of my life but decided to give walking another try just to show that I hadn't lost my spirit.

We made it outside and to the car. It was quiet; the humming of the wide-beamed overhead lights rang through the night air. I shrugged, stuck my finger down my throat, and let loose a thick stream of vomit on the hood of the Audi. My friends, seeing this and getting splashed a little bit, also began to vomit non-ethnocentric chunks all over the car's hood and windshield. And we would have gotten away with it, too, but my friends and I had passed out three, five, and zero feet from the car. When the party was over, the birthday boy got another surprise. He was being a snitch and called his parents, so I panicked. I had a joint in my pocket, so I lit it up, took the biggest hit I could possibly take, and blew it on the birthday boy. His parents arrived a minute later and he smelled heavily of cannabis, which I pointed out. We also said that the birthday boy forced us to smoke marijuana with him, and that it made us vomit because none of us had tried it before. His parents tried to return the car, but the dealership wouldn't accept it because of severe paint damage to the hood, so he got to keep it. He never did thank us.

SKIRT STEAK WITH CHIMICHURRI

If you're an asshole and you drink, I tell you with absolute certainty that you'll do something you'll regret while inebriated. Every terrible person should have a repertoire of alcohol-quashing dishes that will turn your drunk frown into a sober upside-down frown and let you say you're sorry.

3 tablespoons red wine vinegar
2 tablespoons water
4 cloves garlic, minced
½ teaspoon red pepper flakes
½ bay leaf
¼ cup extra-virgin olive oil
½ cup fresh flat-leaf parsley, finely chopped
A skirt steak
Salt and pepper

For the chimichurri, stir together the vinegar, water, garlic, red pepper flakes, and bay leaf. Whisk in the oil and parsley, let it stand for an hour, then throw out the bay leaf, unless you want to choke to death; then keep it. Get your grill hot; dirty talking or a massage that starts as an actual massage but soon turns erotic work well. Coat your steak with lots of salt and pepper and grill it until perfectly done the way you want it. Slice the steak against the grain, put it on a plate—or if you want to be fancy, a serving platter—spoon the chimichurri on top, and serve.

I'M A POSITIVE ROLE MODEL, GODDAMNIT

My whole family knows that I recreationally smoke what scientists call the wacky tobaccy. And at least once during every family gathering, a relative will drop a subtle, "So did you hear that marijuana has been shown to cause male breasts? Another reason not to do it." Then he'd casually look in my direction and ask what my opinion is on that. So it was no surprise that my cousins, all in different stages of high school, came to me to get their weed for the first time.

Well, goddamn it, I may be a terrible person, but I'm a principled terrible person, so I knew it was my responsibility to make sure they didn't try drugs until they were really ready. And since they were asking they must be ready, so it's my cousinly duty to help them acquire drugs. And I did, real sticky stuff, too.

They offered me glaringly wrong amounts of money. My youngest cousin gave me three one-dollar bills, hiding the bills in his palm and slipping them to me in a handshake learned from watching mobsters pay off casino employees in the talkies. My eldest cousin pulled out $120.50 in rolls of quarters; he felt those would be hard to trace, thus were a safe bet. The third cousin just assumed that I'd get him drugs *and* buy him drugs, which was assuredly not the case.

Getting pot when you live in a city is very, very easy. It's comes to you via delivery service, like getting a pizza but with drugs. (NOTE TO SELF: Consider starting a business that delivers drugs *and* pizzas, man.) I got my cousins an eighth for fifty bucks (I know, the prices these days, can you believe it?) and put it in the glove box of my car so that I wouldn't be tempted to smoke it. I was going home for Thanksgiving the next day, where I would see my cousins, give them their pot, and presumably show them how to smoke it because these kids were rubes.

It's a five-hour trip from my home in Brooklyn to where I grew up, upstate. And somewhere in hour two of that trip, my friends who were hitching a ride home found the pot in the glove box. Long story short, we smoked all of it, and the five-hour trip took us nine and a half because we stopped twice for food, and once to try to find more pot, which unfortunately wasn't fruitful.

I knew my cousins were going to be disappointed. I felt I had to come through for them, but I didn't have any way to get pot in our hometown because I'm weak, and where I live, pot comes to me. I scavenged my car for any pot that perhaps I forgot about, which seemed reasonable. I found two blunt roaches and an earring that may have just been a tack. I don't know; I'm not good at jewelry. So I did what any good, principled person would do, and dumped some oregano in a ziptop bag and dropped the roaches in to make it smell like pot.

My cousins were excited. When they arrived at my parents' house for Thanksgiving dinner, they couldn't make eye contact with me without smiling like a war camp refugee seeing sky for the first time after being freed. We went to a big field by the house and they passed around a joint. Only the youngest coughed; the older two had been practicing with joints they made by rolling up chamomile tea. "You know, so we don't look stupid."

After hearing "Do you feel anything?" approximately thirty times in three minutes, they started acting very high. Extremely high. Suddenly I was glad that all telephones were also camcorders and I filmed them. After I was thoroughly embarrassed for them, I told them that they smoked oregano, showed them the video of them acting like asses, and told them that if they ever try buying weed from anyone other than me, I'll put the video on the Internet and ruin them. Customers for life; you can't beat that.

POT BROWNIES

If you are ever in the position of needing to distribute marijuana (let's be honest; we've all been there), it's best to let the post office do the actual drug dealing by mailing pot brownies, provided the post office still exists when this book is published because, let's face it, those guys are fucked.

4 ounces unsweetened chocolate
¾ cup pot butter
¾ cup white sugar
¾ cup brown sugar
¼ cup cocoa powder, unsweetened
½ teaspoon ground cinnamon
3 eggs
2 teaspoons vanilla extract
1 cup all-purpose flour
Pinch of salt

Preheat your oven to 350°F and grease a 9" × 9" square cake pan. In a double boiler, melt the chocolate over medium heat. Stir in the pot butter, which you'll need to figure out how to make and/or acquire on your own because you're a big boy and/or girl. When the butter is incorporated into the chocolate, remove from the heat. In a large bowl, combine the two sugars, cocoa powder, and cinnamon. Add the chocolate and pot butter and stir until combined. Mix in the eggs one at a time, then stir in the vanilla, flour, and salt until smooth. Pour into the greased pan and bake for 35 minutes. Make sure you don't store them out in the open or you'll eat one, get the munchies, and then "oh hey, brownies!" and it's a slippery slope from there.

R. KELLY IS MY NORTH STAR

The Spanish language, and probably other languages (I didn't check), is kind of funny. If a million women are standing together, that group is *ellas*. But if a single man wanders upon the million women (perhaps he's in charge or something), they become *ellos*, a masculine group. When you're doing drugs socially, people who are bad at taking drugs are that sole man amongst a million women; they change the group for everyone.

I had a friend who knew that he was bad at taking drugs. The problem was, many of my friendships were predicated upon a mutual enjoyment of smoking weed and playing video games and/or watching movies, so being the only sober friend made him acutely aware of feeling like an outsider (he was; we could take him or leave him). One night, where marijuana cigarettes were being consumed quite liberally, he had enough and announced that he was going to smoke. The announcement was met with much celebration by all attendees; it was even decided that, in celebration, we would go out for patty melts, which makes sense if you've ever smoked pot before.

Things started well; he took two small hits, finally enjoying the assimilation he so craved. But the limelight proved treacherous, as two small hits became two large hits, and two large hits became two more large hits. Terrible drug friend was very high, becoming almost Asian in his permanent squint resulting from his smile. And as we all put on our shoes to leave for patty melts (we're not imbeciles, no shoes in the house), something changed.

His glee turned to anxiety and he wouldn't go near the door, even when we chanted his name in unison, which usually convinces men to do just about anything.

He was freaking out. We told him that he was fine, that nothing bad was going to happen, and that the weed was only doing exactly what it should be doing so try to enjoy it. He did none of those things; he just sweat a lot and blinked like Jeremiah Denton. I was hungry and dealing with his terrible drug-taking abilities was wearing thin, so I followed the word of America's greatest poet, R. Kelly, and trapped him in a closet. Then I went and got a patty melt.

When we got home, all was quiet. We stared at the closet door in fear and tiptoed over to it cautiously. We unlocked the closet, cautiously opening it in case a pit viper or unreasonably angry friend was ready to strike. Our friend lay there on a pile of coats looking high and very sleepy. "Did you guys get me a patty melt?" We did, but we ate it on the way home. Everyone got a bite but him. In hindsight, I can see why he felt left out.

PATTY MELTS

If you take someone's food, but you know how to replace it with a homemade version, then nothing wrong has transpired.

½ cup butter, divided
1 large onion, sliced
1½ pounds ground beef
Salt and pepper
1 teaspoon Worcestershire sauce
8 slices Swiss cheese
8 slices rye bread

In a sauté pan, melt 2 tablespoons of butter over medium heat. Add the sliced onions and cook slowly for 20 minutes, stirring occasionally, until the onions are soft and caramelized. In a bowl, mix together the ground beef, salt, pepper, and Worcestershire sauce. Form the mixture into four patties. Melt 2 tablespoons of butter in a large sauté pan over medium heat, and cook the patties for 2 to 3 minutes per side, until medium-rare. Each patty gets sandwiched between two pieces of rye, two slices of Swiss, and some onions. Add 2 more tablespoons of butter to the sauté pan and put the assembled sandwiches back in the pan until the cheese starts to melt. Add the last 2 tablespoons of butter to the pan, flip the patty melt, and cook until the cheese is gooey. My God, I almost ended a recipe on the word "gooey." Ridiculous.

GOOD BOY

I like dogs more than humans, but I like humans more than cyborgs. I've always been extremely close to and fiercely protective of my dogs. When I was eight, my parents ran an overnight summer camp and the whole family was there including our wonderful dog Sammy, who would wander around camp and brighten everyone's day through his preciousness. One day, I wandered upon a young lad throwing rocks at my dog, who was swimming like a little angel in the lake. I told him to stop. He did not stop. I put him in a sleeper hold, just like they did on TV, and he stopped skipping stones and also being conscious. I was kicked out of the camp my parents directed because I refused to apologize for defending my dog. This would become repetitive behavior.

My sister was three years ahead of me in school. When she was a senior in high school, I was a freshman, and at the beginning of the school year our aunt died from breast cancer. My parents flew down to help out with funeral arrangements and left us home alone for a few days with my sister in charge. She decided she was going to have a party.

It was going to be amazing, I thought. I would be the only freshman at a party filled with seniors. But it wasn't amazing. Despite their addition of three years, these people hadn't yet learned manners and/or were all unilaterally raised in a barn or other livestock holding structure. I spent most of the evening reminding people to take their shoes off, asking them to use a coaster, and suggesting that they not engage in fellatio on my parents' bed. The party was no fun; I was being forced to act like an adult, so I decided to smoke some pot and relax. I inserted myself into a circle of seniors passing a poorly rolled joint around. When the joint came around, they reluctantly passed it to me, and man, I got zozzled. I couldn't stop smiling and my vision looked like Super 8mm film. I walked inside totally relaxed, eyes barely open, but open enough to see, kneeling in my living room, the abhorrent Josh Katz blowing pot smoke into my dog's face.

When I'm high, I don't feel like fighting. But when I saw that miserable excuse for a human being shotgunning my dog, I didn't feel high. I felt angry. He inhaled again, taking a large hit off of a ridiculous glass bong that was probably purchased at a mall kiosk somewhere terrible, and just as he was about to exhale, I kicked him in the back of the head so hard that I fell backward (he fell forward). He coughed and made choking sounds. I rolled him onto his back and punched him in the face, screaming, "Don't fuck with my dog!" over and over.

I got my ass kicked definitely the worst I've ever had my ass kicked before. I got punched in the eye, mouth, nose, stomach, and dick; kicked in the ribs; thrown down the stairs to my front porch; and spit on. I knew I couldn't take on Josh Katz and all of his friends, so I did the next best thing. I called the cops to break up the party, and poured a full pound of sugar in Josh Katz's gas tank, which ruined his fancy Jew car. I've never told anyone about the car thing, but I checked and the statute of limitations has expired so ha, fuck you, Josh Katz. I ruined your car, you fucking jerk.

BACON EGG AND CHEESE WITH SRIRACHA AIOLI

Fighting is almost never the answer, unless the question is: "What is an active tense synonym for brouhaha?" If you fight for a worthy cause and lose, do something nice for yourself. And if we're to believe cereal commercials, a great day starts with breakfast, so do that or something.

Some bacon
Some eggs
A lot of butter
Some sort of bread-like product
Some American cheese
1 egg yolk
1 tablespoon lemon juice
1 teaspoon water
1 teaspoon Dijon mustard
1 cup olive oil
3 tablespoons sriracha
Salt and pepper

Cook the bacon, cook the eggs with lots of butter, place both on one half of bread-like product, and top with American cheese. Using a blender, combine the egg yolk, lemon juice, water, and mustard, or if you're fancy and short on space, use an immersion blender. Slowly add the olive oil and continue to blend, until the mixture becomes mayo-like. Add the sriracha, and then season with salt and pepper to taste. Slather the other half of the bread-like product in mayo, eat the sandwich, and start feeling better.

PRISONER, FOR AN EVENING

I grew up forty miles from a super-max prison. It housed murderers, rapists, serial killers, all sorts of bad dudes. It was in a small rural town filled with trailers sitting on big lots, and everyone who lived there worked either at the prison or the ski hill nearby.

I frequented that ski hill daily during the winter. My friends and I would meet there after school and ski or snowboard until they closed at 9:00 P.M. If the ski hill was a diner and not a ski hill, we would have been able to walk in, get jovially greeted (by our Christian names), "order the usual," and get exactly what we had hoped for. The employees liked us because my friend sold most of them weed (and sometimes ecstasy). Most of them were young people just unlucky to be born in the middle of fucking nowhere. Some were adults with less than the median number of teeth, working two jobs just to put food on the table. Some were Jews from the nearby wealthy city that were too cheap to buy a season's pass for their family, so instead they sold themselves off into indentured servitude to save a couple hundred bucks. One of the groomers was a prison guard by day. He groomed the slopes because it cleared his head, allowed him to relax and unwind. He would smoke a joint, get in the snowcat, and forget all about the violence and horror he sees at his other job. And he just so happened to buy his weed from my best friend, so he liked us the most out of all of 'em.

We ran into him one night as he pulled up in his truck. In the passenger seat were a half dozen brand-new prison jumpsuits. We asked him why he had them and he told us that he steals them and sells them so he has cash to buy weed. Being a pragmatist, I brought up Marx's theory of money as the universal commodity and suggested we simply exchange jumpsuits for the bubonic chronic, and that's how we came to have official Attica prison jumpsuits. We just had to promise that we wouldn't wear them anywhere near the prison, which of course we agreed to.

That night, we drove two exits down the New York State Thruway to Attica. We got high in the parking lot of a nearby Denny's and slipped on the jumpsuits. We sauntered into the casual family dining restaurant, expecting the patrons and proprietor to react with great fear, at which point we'd reveal that we aren't *actually* prisoners; we're just four clever lads *pretending* to be prisoners. Then we'd all share a hearty laugh for pulling such a quick one on them, and in thanks for the terrific entertainment we'd get our dinners comped, and maybe also ice cream. But they didn't even seem to notice. We enjoyed our meal, which was both filling as well as an everyday good value, and went back out to the car, disappointed that we didn't get the attention we so desperately craved.

We had to step up our game. We drove half a mile from the prison and pulled the car over. The highway was 200 feet in front of us. We could see a large green and white exit sign bearing the words "Attica Correctional Facility" with an arrow pointed just off the road. We got out of the car and ran to the sign. One by one, we would run in front of cars, then dive into the median and pretend to be running for our lives. Three cars spun out, but were unscathed; two others drove off the road, but their cars weren't that damaged.

Before we could pull onto the highway, three police cars descended upon us. Officers in black tactical gear stood behind their doors with their weapons drawn and yelled a bunch of stuff.

They really took their time sorting things out. It felt like they were doing it intentionally, really. We explained that it was a comedy of errors, with an emphasis on the comedy, but they had us lie down on the snowy ground with guns pointed at us as they checked our IDs. Finally, after twenty-five minutes (that comes out to five minutes per ID check, which seems flagrantly excessive) they confirmed that we were in fact handsome rascals up to clever mischief and not actual incarcerated miscreants, and let us go. But not before giving us some boring lecture about public safety, and just generally not being respectful of our time. Don't worry; they didn't get away with it. I lodged a formal complaint.

WEISSEN SOUR

If you want people to forget about the stupid things you've done, help them forget with alcohol. Unless they're alcoholics; then just use roofies (or alcohol).

2 ounces bourbon
¾ ounce fresh lemon juice
¼ ounce simple syrup
½ teaspoon orange marmalade
2 dashes orange bitters
2 ounces white ale

Combine all of the ingredients into a shaker with ice and gently shake for about 10 seconds. Strain into a highball glass with ice cubes, and garnish with lemon or something.

CHAPTER 10

"God"

THE POLYGAMOUS HITCHHIKER

For two winters and springs, I lived in Salt Lake City, Utah, which was not very wonderful. Utah is a shithole, and if there were a waterborne additive that forced chemical castration, I'd suggest we put it in their water supply to inhibit any Utahan (see, even their demonym is annoying) from procreating, thereby eradicating the pimple on the otherwise flawless complexion of the United States of America. But that doesn't exist, so no point in getting your hopes up.

Picking up a hitchhiker is usually a terrible idea; even if your passenger prescribes to the 14th Constitutional Amendment, "Ass, grass, or gas, nobody rides for free . . ." the potential dangers of non-simulated rape, chainsaw-related death, or overall stranger danger are very real. But in Utah, you can throw all that out the window; Utah is one of the safest places on earth. Even if statistics don't back that up (they may; I'll be honest I didn't check), nobody is scary in Utah by the very fact that they're in Utah. My hitchhiker passed the safety test; he was white, was in Utah, and wasn't wielding a chainsaw or large menacing erection.

He was walking casually on the road's shoulder, thumb raised and held outward. I pulled my car over and he got in the passenger seat. The problem with Mormons is that they live among us without us even knowing; they can look like just about anyone (well, anyone white). We made polite small talk and nothing seemed to be out of the ordinary. The snow was coming down hard and the wind was whipping it around the winding mountain pass, making it difficult to see. We fell into a comfortable silence as I focused on the road. I could feel his stare; I didn't know whether he was trying to assess the rape situation or wanted to sit on my lap and drive because his father was never "there" for him, but I didn't like it. The roads were getting worse and now I had proper vehicle safety and the hitchhiker that I probably shouldn't have picked up in the first place to worry about.

"Do you mind if I ask you a question?" He just did. "What is your relationship with the lord and savior, Jesus Christ?"

"That's not something I'm going to talk about with you," I said.

"Well, what do you know about the Mormon religion?" he asked.

I turned, doing my best Burt Reynolds steely gaze that says, "I may look calm, but I mean business," and told him, "If you insist upon talking about religion, I'll insist upon removing you from my automobile, posthaste!"

He was silent for a few minutes. I drove cautiously along the narrow road, doing my best not to peek over the cliff protected by a flimsy rusted guardrail. "It's obvious that Satan has clouded your heart and mind so that you're unable to see the truth of the gospel." This is why people hate Mormons. I should have said that. Damn, that would have been a sick burn.

I pulled the car onto the road's shoulder, got out, and pulled him from the passenger seat. It was getting dark and the weather conditions were not hospitable. "You can't leave me here. I could die out here," he pleaded.

"You shouldn't have talked about religion."

"Please. I'm sorry."

"I'm sorry, too, but rules are rules." I walked around the front of the car and got back in. In the distance, an SUV lost its grip on the roadway and barreled into the rocky mountainside. Cars slammed their brakes to avoid the SUV, causing a chaotic sea of sliding cars. I noticed how warm the seat heaters felt against my butt cheeks. The Mormon appeared next to my window, pleading with me.

"This is a judgment upon your character," he said. "This is a judgment, upon your character." Goddamn it. I let him back in the car, but not before locking the door at the exact moment he tried to open it approximately seven times. He was now more afraid of me than I was of him, which is the only way to ensure your safety when picking up a hitchhiker. But if you traumatize them to the point of tears, as in my case, it's considered proper to feed them; it helps the body cope with shock, especially if you don't want them to do voodoo on you (or whatever black magic they practice).

MAI TAI

Apologies don't have to be sincere, so food-based apologies shouldn't have to be, either. Sometimes it's the perfect excuse to slip meat into a vegetarian friend's food, or trick a Mormon into committing an atrocity toward God by drinking alcohol with a classic Tiki drink.

¾ ounce fresh lime juice
¼ ounce rock candy syrup
¼ ounce Orgeat almond syrup
½ ounce orange curaçao
2 ounces aged rum
Fresh mint sprig

Add the lime juice, rock candy syrup, Orgeat syrup, curaçao, and aged rum to a shaker and fill with crushed ice. Shake vigorously until the shaker is well chilled and frosty on the outside and your poor little hands can't take it anymore. Pour, unstrained, into an old-fashioned glass, and garnish with a sprig of mint.

NEVER TRUST A MAN IN A SPORT SANDAL

When I was fourteen, I went to a Catholic sleepaway camp. And not because I was interested in Catholicism, but because I had already been kicked out of the two Jewish camps in the area. Being the token Jew at a Catholic summer camp, the possibility of being an asshole was not only omnipresent but taunting me at every juncture. I had tried to be on my best behavior after I learned that Catholic girls compartmentalized virginity and anal virginity into two separate and not equal categories.

I'm barely Jewish. It's not that I'm ashamed of it—in fact, I exploit it for everything it's worth—but I never went to temple, don't believe in God, and don't have cloven-hoofed feet. Yet despite that, I managed to single myself out as "different" amongst an otherwise Christian crowd. I was happy being the outcast Jew; it seemed like a good character role from a really progressive film in the 1950s.

Breakfast began at 8:00 A.M. on every day but Sunday, when the Lord insists that an additional hour of sleep must be taken in His name. "Please stand for the morning prayer," boomed over the microphone, held by a man in Tevas whom I'm assuming was named something like Sig or Tad or something terrible. I grew up to believe that you never listen to a man in a sport sandal; my dad didn't like them, and his dad didn't like them, and damn it I didn't like them. A cross between a sneaker and a sandal? Come on, Teva, you're not fooling anyone.

I didn't want to stand; partially because I don't like praying, but mostly because it was early and I hadn't had my coffee. The other campers dutifully rose around me, forming a Christian barrier that I thought would protect me from being seen seated. "We'll wait for everyone to stand." Heads started turning, looking to identify the offender who was delaying their meal.

For most teenagers, being the center of attention is a fate worse than walking in on one of your parents' wrestle naps, but I was used to being the center of negative attention; this was my sweet spot.

Sport Sandals was determined to wait. The prayer, and subsequent meal, would not proceed until I was standing. "Everyone is waiting on you," he kept saying, like I was hard of hearing. I was at a not-literal crossroads: stand for fifteen seconds and get on with my day, or be a huge asshole and let it ride.

"Prove God exists and I'll stand."

Boom.

They kicked me out. Not for not standing to pray to a God that I don't believe exists, although that probably didn't help the situation. I got kicked out because I called the "cool," "hip," Teva-wearing youth pastor a Holocaust denier and mocked his choice of footwear, which he called "as versatile as it is fashionable."

It was a two-hour drive home, on mostly straight roads past farms, fields, and depressed rust-belt towns. My parents were camp directors by profession and their son had been kicked out of all the camps in the area; heck, I had been kicked out of their camp twice. They didn't say anything on the car ride home, but when they picked me up from camp,

the Christian camp director recognized them from a camping conference, and I'll never forget what they said to her: "We're much better
with other people's children." Sick burn.

FRIED CHICKEN

If you're really, really sorry, make fried chicken. Unless you're apologizing for being racist toward black people; then it might just come off as offensive. But in literally all other cases, fried chicken.

2 tablespoons kosher salt, divided

2 tablespoons freshly ground black pepper, divided

1½ teaspoons smoked paprika

¾ teaspoon cayenne pepper

½ teaspoon garlic powder

½ teaspoon onion powder

3–4 pounds chicken, broken down

1 cup buttermilk

1 large egg

½ cup water

3 cups all-purpose flour

1 tablespoon cornstarch

Peanut oil

Honey

Hot sauce

Whisk half of the salt, half of the black pepper, paprika, cayenne, garlic powder, and onion powder in a small bowl. Rub the spices all over the chicken, then cover and chill overnight. Whisk the buttermilk, egg, and water in a medium bowl. In a baking dish, combine the flour, cornstarch, and remaining salt and pepper. One piece at a time, dip the chicken in the buttermilk mixture, allowing the excess to drip back into the bowl, then dredge in the flour mixture, shaking off the excess. Fry the chicken in peanut oil, turning with tongs every 1 to 2 minutes and adjusting heat to maintain a steady temperature of 300°F to 325°F. Fry until the skin is golden brown, about 10 minutes for wings and 12 minutes for thighs, legs, and tittays. Serve with honey and hot sauce.

BIBLICAL TORTURE PORN

The Catholic Church, for being one of the most well-funded, evangelized organizations in the history of the world, has sure gotten away with some shit. The Crusades, the Inquisitions, Witch Hunts, Holocaust-denying popes, doing nothing about the whole rampant child molestation then buying the victims' silence thing; you know, just to name a few. And while clearly all or even most Catholics aren't bad, when you're an asshole details like that don't matter.

When I was fifteen, my parents took a trip over Christmas vacation on which I was not invited. Smartly, they didn't allow me to stay home alone, unwilling to make the same mistakes the McCallisters made by leaving little Kevin. It was decided that I'd stay with my friend's family and celebrate Christmas with them.

Things were going swimmingly. My parents were vacationing happily; I was getting my first taste of Christmas; and Macaulay Culkin was battling deep-seated substance abuse issues likely related to being a child star. It was announced that in my temporary family, it was tradition to go to Mass on Christmas; I thought that Boston was a fairly long drive from upstate New York, but who doesn't like a road trip? But I was mistaken. Mass was not shorthand for a state filled with second-class bandwagon sports fans; it's a thing at a church where an old guy talks for what seems like forever and people make noises in unison.

Somewhere between getting scolded for taking Communion despite actively denying the existence of God and "disrupting" some preachy lady because I was snoring, I took a bathroom break. I was told the bathroom was down the long hallway decorated with religious torture porn, then a quick left, then it's the second door on the right. On the way back from the bathroom, I passed a door that had "Priest's Office" painted on the glass, like an old-timey PI. Surreptitiously, I tried the doorknob. It was unlocked.

The priest's office was decorated sparsely: an old carved wooden desk, a wall of ancient books, and a Gateway desktop computer that probably came in a cow-patterned cardboard box. The computer glowed majestically; beams of light surrounded it and everything in my periphery glowed in soft focus. It was my burning bush and must have been God's way of telling me to look up some messed-up porn on the priest's computer; you know, just for laughs, but also to bring to light the church's poor handling of the molestation cases, if people could see beyond the humor.

I didn't want to look up kiddie porn because that just seemed a little too real, so I settled on some good old-fashioned barnyard pornography, in which a consenting adult performer has sex with a consenting horse, goat, pig, or field mouse. Then I checked my e-mail, played Minesweeper, and re-joined my temporary family just as Mass was winding down.

The next morning, I anxiously awoke, eager to open Christmas presents for the first time in my life. I violently shook my friend awake and we made our way downstairs to the tree. His mother was already downstairs, sitting on the edge of the couch, sobbing gently and silently into a tissue. She had on the news and there was a breaking story; her beloved priest was being investigated for distributing lewd and illegal acts.

I came clean, eventually. I had to give a public apology, complete 120 hours of community service, and I was told it was very likely that the priest would press charges against me and my family in civil court, but he never did. Man, those guys are forgiving.

BODY OF CHRIST CRUSTED SCALLOPS
WITH BEURRE ROUGE

Some dishes you make for forgiveness. This one is crusted in forgiveness, or at least the "body" of a guy who was apparently, like, super forgiving.

¾ cup red wine vinegar
¾ cup Zinfandel or other dry red wine
½ cup minced shallots
2 fresh tarragon sprigs, plus extra for garnish
½ teaspoon whole white or black peppercorns

½ cup butter, cut into 6 pieces, plus 2 teaspoons butter reserved
Salt and pepper
12 Communion wafers
16 sea scallops
2 tablespoons olive oil

Combine the vinegar, wine, shallots, tarragon, and peppercorns in a small saucepan. Boil until the mixture is reduced to ¼ cup, about 20 minutes, then strain. Return the liquid to the saucepan and simmer over medium-low heat. Whisk in the butter, 1 piece at a time, whisking constantly and allowing each piece to melt before adding the next. The sauce should be smooth and creamy; if the butter breaks, throw it out and do it again. Season the sauce to taste with salt and pepper and remove from the heat. Add the Communion wafers and a pinch of salt and pepper to a food processor. Pulse until it has a sandy texture, and then coat both sides of each scallop with the mixture. In a sauté pan, heat the olive oil over high heat until it smokes, then add the scallops. Cook until just opaque in the center, about 1 minute per side, then add the remaining butter into the pan and spoon it over the scallops, not assume the intercoursing pos. Serve the scallops with the beurre rouge, garnish with fresh tarragon, and feel the power of delicious compel you.

MY VERY FIRST COMMUNION

It was a bit dry and very bland. It was also a bit confusing; the whole transubstantiation thing still doesn't make a whole lot of sense to me. I had just eaten the body of Christ for the first time; I was at church with my friend's family, who had invited me to spend Easter with them and neglected to mention the religious component of their celebration.

My friend watched me eat the wafer and waited until afterward to explain that I had just literally eaten the body of Christ. We bickered over his use of the word "literally." I alleged that he was literally using "literally" in the literal opposite way it was intended to be used. He explained that many Christians believe that once the priest has prayed over the cheese and crackers or whatever it is, they *literally* are the blood and body of Christ, no matter how much science and linguistics would disagree. I assured him that his knowledge of human physiology was astoundingly poor if he believed that generic body was made available in cracker form. Fed up, he briefed his mother on the situation and asked her to explain to me how the Eucharist works.

She seemed very upset that I had eaten Christ. She looked around the church and made eye contact with a deacon, then motioned for him to come over. Suddenly my ingestion of the tasteless little cracker had become the business of all the nosey church people. People began whispering; I became a distraction to the service.

The deacon was a reasonable man, pragmatic even. He simply said, "For it to be a mortal sin, the sinner must know that he is doing something wrong. That is clearly not the case." Everyone breathed a not-literal collective sigh of relief and the service continued without interruption, for a while.

I sat in the pew, which kept making me laugh because it reminded me of laser fights, "pew, pew pew pew." I couldn't stop thinking about how I had figuratively, not literally, eaten a human being and washed it down with the liquid of his exsanguination. I felt queasy, gassy even. Then we came to the portion of the service when people are supposed to stand and sit with irregular continuity, and it pushed me over the edge.

I had an aisle seat, so when I vomited it didn't hit anyone directly, but it did make it very easy for everyone to see the small pile of pinkish throw-up staining the carpeted aisle. Sitting amongst the small orange pile were the unmistakable markings of the Jesus cracker. The deacon saw this and made a surprised sound like he orgasmed, which I hope he didn't because I think they have to swear to God to not ejaculate or something. One by one, churchgoer heads swung around, necks craned to get a look at the commotion. There were whisperings that I needed to re-ingest Jesus. Then somebody argued that I shouldn't have eaten not-literal him in the first place, because, you know, I'm Jewish, so I certainly shouldn't eat it again. Then somebody started throwing around the word "miracle," claiming that Jesus eradicated himself from my stomach for being a non-believer. The church went quiet as the priest walked from the stage to examine the pile of literal vomit. He looked at me with grave disappointment and I said, "Kind of ironic that this happened on Easter. I literally resurrected Jesus from my stomach." The joke didn't kill, but it got some laughs.

NACHO CHEESE EUCHARIST

Jesus tastes a lot better when he's Jesús, so make nacho cheese–flavored Eucharist to apologize for any Christian-related sins.

1¼ cups all-purpose flour
¼ cup nacho cheese powder
½ teaspoon salt
2 tablespoons canola oil
4–8 tablespoons water

Preheat your oven to 400°F. In a food processor, combine the flour, nacho cheese powder, salt, and oil. Pulse, adding water 1 tablespoon at a time until the mixture forms a small ball. On a floured work surface, roll the dough until ⅛" thick and then cut crackers out with a cookie cutter of your choosing. Bake on a sheet tray lined with parchment paper for 12 minutes. Serve with a glass of wine.

ANTI-VAX

When I was twenty-four, I volunteered at a children's hospital. Okay, more accurately, I was once given a judge-mandated 120 hours of community service for a nasty little misunderstanding between me, some fire, and a couple of houses, so I served that 120 hours at the hospital. They apparently viewed volunteer work as a form of punishment, so they had me work on humdrum tasks like filing and data entry rather than performing surgery and chatting up patients with my patented brand of comical but also informational bedside manner like I had thought they would.

One day, I heard two Jamaican nurses gossiping in the break room about how a patient's mother refused to have her child vaccinated because she believed it caused autism. They were talking about how the ignorant mother and her child were a danger to mankind, how people like her and her ticking time bomb of a child could compromise herd immunity, and reintroduce diseases that smart people have learned to control. And worst of all, this mother was steadfast in her views because she heard them from Jenny McCarthy, who the Jamaican nurses kept referring to as "that dumb white bitch."

The woman began handing out informational pamphlets in front of the hospital promoting "Generation Rescue," an organization run by that dumb white bitch that promotes "rescuing" children from vaccinations, and also probably eventually measles, polio, and all of the other diseases that will come back if people stop vaccinating their stupid children. She was causing quite the stir, and doctors would pedantically detail why anti-vaccination people are the second-worst people in the world, right behind New England Patriots fans; nurses would throw HIPPA rules aside and gossip about which patients were anti-vaxxers; and a janitor told me that he once took a shit in a bedpan just to see how it felt, which isn't really on topic but was also interesting (he said it felt exciting).

One day, toward the end of my required 120 hours, I heard the nurses gossiping that the son of the woman who passed out anti-vaccination pamphlets was back in the hospital. Since they had me doing data entry, I had access to all patient files as well as a floor plan showing which patients were in which rooms. I went to the bathroom, changed into street clothes, stuffed my hospital-mandated work wear in the garbage (never leave a trace), and went to room 314.

He was a quiet kid. He had the air of someone who had experienced great trauma early on in life and would grow up strong and stoic until he got into an accident with nuclear waste, at which point he'd acquire magical powers and then avenge whatever haunted him from his child-hood. In this case, it was having a batshit crazy mother. I had planned on trying to talk some sense into the child, hoping that he could convince his mother that it was okay to be vaccinated, but he was only two years old and I'm not comfortable talking to children. I was about to leave, but a nurse came in and asked with great hope and optimism if I was the father.

Yes . . . yes, of course I am. She smiled and immediately launched into a rant about how I should really vaccinate my child, but I interrupted her and demanded that she vaccinate my child right this instant, the sooner the better. She rushed out of the room, and half a minute later the doctor returned, eagerly pricking the young boy with a variety of needles so that I couldn't change my mind.

The kid didn't even cry. His mom did, though. I don't feel the least bit bad about this one. Get your children vaccinated. Also, get your pets spayed and neutered. Also, wipe until it's white.

FRENCH 75

Assholes often save the world. If you watch an end-of-the-world movie, chances are the character saving the world, or the actor (never actress), will be a huge, gaping asshole. So to these great assholes, we honor you, and raise our glasses in celebration.

2 ounces dry gin
1 teaspoon superfine sugar
½ ounce lemon juice
5 ounces champagne

Pour all of the ingredients except the champagne into a cocktail shaker filled with ice. Shake for about 10 seconds. Strain into a collins glass half-filled with cracked ice and top off with champagne.

ABOUT THE AUTHOR

Zach Golden is a great American who is very upset that they canceled *Law & Order*. His childhood was spent in Rochester, New York being raised by wolves then subsequently dolphins then subsequently supermodels. He currently lives in Brooklyn, New York with his wife Sara and dog Oscar, both of whom he allows on the furniture. He enjoys dogs more than humans, but enjoys humans more than robots. You can visit his website at *www.zachgolden.com*.